The sermon exc[...]
servant of God w[...]
his preaching, cor[...]
depth and application, prepared by
the Holy Spirit and study. The international concern and scope of
Dr. Culbertson's ministry are emphasized by the places all around
the world where his messages were
delivered.

For those who have shared in
William Culbertson's life and ministry as students or friends of MBI,
this book will be particularly special. With him we can walk the
corridors of the school and see
changes wrought by his influence – on the physical plant, in the
academic program, with regard to
the wider Institute ministries. And
yet we never doubt the loyal and
immovable defense of the authoritative Word of God that he maintained.

The power of a life lived with
the intent of ending well for God
is captured in this biography. I was
challenged and moved by my reading as I shared in the life of a man
who so succinctly summarized
his working philosophy of life at
the announcement of his election
as president, "I want to be in the
place God wants me to be." –
*Reviewed by Ruth Bruckner, a
Moody graduate who had a special
relationship with the Culbertson family. She interviewed Dr. Culbertson
several times, visited the home on a
number of occasions and worked
closely with Mrs. Culbertson in
gathering material for a "this is your
life" salute to Dr. Culbertson by
MBI students. She is now a student
at Wheaton College.*

William Culbertson:
A Man of God

By

Warren W. Wiersbe

MOODY PRESS
CHICAGO

TO
his wife,
Catharine Culbertson,
and his secretary,
May Hogan,
who were, as he would have said,
"Women which labored with me in the gospel."

"My first impression and the lasting one is that he is a man of God."

WILBUR M. SMITH
"Culbertson Day"
May 19, 1971

Contents

5

Foreword

In death, there is a time for silence and a time for words. This is the time to pay tribute to a great departed Christian leader, William Culbertson. Of Abraham Lincoln, it was said, "A tree is best measured when it is down." Dr. Culbertson's reputation had spread far and near as a Bible teacher, educator, administrator, and saint of God.

When we think of our beloved friend and partner, a number of thoughts come to mind. Above all, he was godly. He reminded us, who knew him well, of a tree planted by God. More than anything else in this life, he wanted to please the Lord. His lifelong friend, Edwin Bustard, said of him, "He never caused the enemies of the Lord to blaspheme because of misconduct." His whole nature cried out to know Christ better. Continually, he would encourage the students to go deeper with God.

I believe that Dr. Culbertson was the humblest man I have ever met. Often he quoted John 15:5, "Without me ye can do nothing." He constantly underestimated himself and overestimated others. When he was chosen to become the president of the Institute, he was very surprised. "Very frankly," he said, "I didn't have in mind the presidency. I was satisfied in the field of education. I didn't feel qualified at all to be president." He even tried to resign once.

Dr. Culbertson was steadfast and courageous. Though gracious and gentle, he held firm convictions. He loved the Word of God passionately and wholeheartedly embraced the fundamentals of the faith.

7

He had compassion besides intelligence, which is a rare combination. It was this passion that excited and united men and women at the Moody Bible Institute to purposeful action.

Dr. Culbertson was godly, humble, steadfast, loving, intelligent, and always abounding in the work of the Lord. His final parting verse to us was Revelation 19:6, "Alleluia: for the Lord God omnipotent reigneth."

Warren Wiersbe, at our request, has written the biography of this great servant of God. The author has caught the spirit of William Culbertson and told the story well. It is with love and prayer that I commend this book to you.

DR. GEORGE SWEETING
President
Moody Bible Institute

Preface

The Moody Bible Institute and the Culbertson family requested that this book not be a "definitive biography." They wanted a personal account of Dr. Culbertson's life and ministry that would be an encouragement and challenge to other Christians, and this is what I have attempted to write. This explains the absence of footnotes and the galaxy of details that would bore even the closest relatives.

However, I have tried to be careful in details, even though they have not been documented in the text. I have filed with Moody Press an annotated copy of the manuscript, together with the original source materials, or copies of the originals. Some future biographer or historian with a flair for footnotes can examine these sources to his heart's content.

My three chief sources of information have been Mrs. Catharine Culbertson and the members of the family; Miss May Hogan, and Dr. Culbertson's correspondence and files at the Moody Bible Institute. I have interviewed scores of people and corresponded with others, and have listened many times to tapes of the important events of his official career, where such tapes were available. I also read dozens and dozens of Dr. Culbertson's sermons, radio messages, and chapel talks, as well as the "Man to Man" record series. He was not given to opening his heart to just anyone, yet it is amazing how often he opened his heart in his sermons.

After I came to Moody Church, September 1, 1971, Dr. and Mrs. Culbertson were often in my congregation. He was a great listener—and a great encourager! I was privileged to visit him often while he was in the hospital; and, for some reason, during those visits, he sometimes bared his heart and shared matters that he had not told many others. I could not claim to be an intimate friend, so it was not that which impelled him. Perhaps it was providential: several of the personal things he told me have found their way into these pages; others will have to remain unpublished.

It would be impossible to name all the people at the Moody Bible Institute who assisted in the gathering of material. I especially wish to thank the Institute for permission to quote from *The Faith Once Delivered* (Moody Press, 1972), *Moody Monthly,* and the "Man to Man" recordings. The staff at Moody Press was also very cooperative and encouraging. They realize that it is not easy to pastor a city church and write a biography at the same time. Grateful thanks are extended to Marshall, Morgan, and Scott, of London, publishers of the messages of the British Keswick convention, for the excerpts quoted from various sermons delivered there by Dr. Culbertson.

I feel that Dr. Culbertson deserves a better book than I have written, but if this is as much help to the reader as it has been to the writer, I will be happy. I feel as though I have been walking on holy ground.

May all of us, as Dr. Culbertson so fervently prayed for himself, end well.

Essential Dates

1905: November 18, birth in Philadelphia, Pennsylvania
1924: Graduation from West Philadelphia High School and entrance into the Reformed Episcopal Seminary, Philadelphia
1927: April 17, start of first pastorate, Grace Reformed Episcopal Church, Collingdale, Pennsylvania
May 19, graduation from seminary and ordination as deacon
1928: Start of teaching at the Philadelphia School of the Bible and also at the Reformed Episcopal Seminary
1929: March 16, marriage to Catharine Gantz
1930: October 1, start of second pastorate, St. John's-by-the-Sea, Ventnor, New Jersey
1933: May 1, start of third pastorate, Church of the Atonement, Germantown, Philadelphia
1937: Election as bishop of the New York and Philadelphia synod, Reformed Episcopal Church
1939: Graduation from Temple University, Philadelphia
Receipt of honorary doctor of divinity degree from the Reformed Episcopal Seminary
1942: September 1, beginning of ministry as dean of education, Moody Bible Institute
1947: June 14, death of Dr. Will H. Houghton
June 19, appointment as acting president of the Institute
1948: February 4, election by the trustees as president of the Institute

11

May 13, official inauguration as president

September, beginning of chairmanship of the advisory board, American Association for Jewish Evangelism

1952:   First trip to the Holy Land

1954:   First ministry at British Keswick

1957:   First missionary trip

1963:   First surgery

1970:   June 14, second surgery

September 22, dedication of Culbertson Hall, men's dormitory

1971:   May 19, Recognition by students, "Culbertson Day"

August 1, start of ministry as chancellor

September 28, inauguration as chancellor; Dr. George Sweeting's inauguration as president

October 6, last trip to the hospital

November 16, homegoing

November 18, memorial service and burial

ONE

The Student

"Young man, how would you like to multiply your life a thousand times?"

The question was blunt, but Dr. J. Davis Adams wanted it to be that way. He was recruiting a new teacher for his Philadelphia School of the Bible, and he knew that the pastor, only twenty-two years old, would respond only to a spiritual challenge. And all the pastor could do was blurt out that he was willing to have his life multiplied a thousand times for God's glory, and that settled it. William Culbertson, pastor of the Grace Reformed Episcopal Church, Collingdale, Pennsylvania, began a teaching ministry at the Philadelphia School of the Bible—a ministry that lasted fourteen years and ultimately led him to the Moody Bible Institute of Chicago.

It was only right that his teaching ministry should begin in Philadelphia, because that is where the whole story begins. William Culbertson was born in Philadelphia on November 18, 1905, the only child of William and Lydia Roper Culbertson. His name had to be William—"just plain William," he used to say—because that was a family tradition, reaching back at least six generations. Great-grandfather Culbertson was the first of the family to come to the United States from Ireland, arriving in the early 1800s and settling down in Philadelphia. His son, William, was born in 1839. He served in the Civil War with the 29th Pennsylvania Volunteers, and in 1871, his son, William, was born. It was this William who, on October 24, 1900, married Lydia Roper, and who fathered Dr. William Culbertson, bishop of the New York and Philadelphia Synod of the Reformed Episcopal Church, and for twenty-three years, president of the Moody Bible Institute of Chicago.

The Culbertson family was average in every way except one: they were known for their practical godliness. They attended the J. Addison Henry Memorial Presbyterian Church in West Philadelphia. In 1924, when young "Bill" applied for admission into the Reformed Episcopal Seminary in Philadelphia, one of his former pastors, Henry E. Jones, wrote to the committee,

> His parents are two of the most godly people I ever knew. Father was an honored and most faithful Elder in my church. Mother a loving and zealous worker in church and Sabbath School. Blood, home-training, church life, combined in a wholesome and gracious influence over the life of their only child—William. In him are all the mental and spiritual qualifications that are essential in a minister whom God can use with power.

It is not surprising that William and Lydia Culbertson's son trusted Christ early in life. "As a lad of nine, tenderly I was led to Him," he wrote in a personal testimony in 1953, "and I found Him all for which a soul could long." His decision was made at an evangelistic meeting, and it was so real to him, that he invited his uncle to accept Christ too. The man responded to God's gracious call, and Bill Culbertson won his first soul to Christ.

Bill was a quiet child whose religious interests were very strong. As soon as he learned to read, he started reading the Bible; and he gladly accompanied his parents and aunt to the services at "Addison Henry." A letter written to his father in 1913 indicates his interests in church—and also his boyish problems with spelling.

> Dear Father
> I am going to school in the morning. Mothier made me a nice new linen suit. I went to church this morning and sat down in front. Mothier said I was a good boy. Aunt Aggie and Aunt Ellie and Uncle Albert was thiere. I went to S.S. this afternoon. Your loving son,
>
> William

He was not a robust child; in fact, he had several falls and broken bones, and some of his friends called him "Billy Brittle Bones." As he entered his teens, he was tall, thin, and a bit stoop shouldered; but what he lacked in weight he made up for in hair. His hair was thick and ruddy, with waves that made people wonder whether the effect had been achieved with a curling iron.

In January 1919, Harold S. Laird became pastor at Addison Henry and, during his five years there, exerted tremendous spiritual influence over Bill Culbertson. He noted that the boy was always in the services, that he took notes on the messages, and that he was a leader among the young people in the church. One of Bill's closest friends was Fred Noble, who had been led to Christ under Pastor Laird's ministry. Bill and Fred were both leaders in the Christian Endeavor program of the church, and, along with Ross McCloy and Howard Criswell, met once a week at the church for prayer and scripture memorization. They met in an "upper room" and seriously tried to encourage one another in the Christian life. Often, Bill and Fred would take walks in Morris Park and discuss the Bible or go over memory verses; and

sometimes, Bill would study his Greek. Interestingly, during
the four years he attended the West Philadelphia High
School, he was able to take Greek. After he graduated in
1924, the course was dropped!

During his teen years, Bill worked in the Acme Stores, a
grocery chain in Philadelphia. Even as a teenager, William
Culbertson made decisions cautiously, a trait that followed
him all his life. He always wanted to be sure of the will of
God, and he believed that God would reveal His will in His
own time if only he would wait. He and Fred took turns
preaching at a mission and leading the church prayer meetings when Pastor Laird was absent. The encouragement and
influence of this loving local church would pay great spiritual dividends in both of their lives in years to come.

Bill was about sixteen when somebody introduced him to
Catharine Gantz, a young lady whose family had just started
attending the church. Her parents, like Bill's, were very
godly people whose convictions about the Word of God had
brought them under Pastor Laird's ministry. All Catharine
noticed when she was introduced was a thin, young man
with a lot of wavy hair. Later, she discovered that there
were brains under those waves, and that Bill Culbertson
was a devoted Christian with a healthy sense of humor and
a love for boyish pranks. Several of the young men in the
church became interested in Catharine Gantz, one of them
quite seriously; but the Lord had chosen her for Bill Culbertson.

Under Pastor Laird's ministry, he had felt a call from God
into Christian service, and he applied to the Reformed Episcopal Seminary in Philadelphia. His mother had been raised
in the Reformed Episcopal Church; and after Pastor Laird
left Addison Henry, Bill's parents had united with a local
Reformed Episcopal congregation. Another influence in his
decision was his mother's former pastor, Dr. Tracy, who suggested that he consider the Reformed Episcopal church.

Bill made an appointment to meet Robert L. Rudolph, the presiding bishop of the Philadelphia and New York synod, and a member of the board of trustees and the faculty of the school.

When Bill arrived at the bishop's apartment building, he came face-to-face with something he had never had to manage before — a self-service elevator. "I don't know how to run that confounded thing!" he said to himself, and proceeded to walk up the stairs to the bishop's third-floor apartment.

"Why did you *walk* up?" Bishop Rudolph asked him. "Why didn't you use the elevator?"

Bill gave him an honest answer, the only kind he knew how to give: "I've never run one of those things, and—I'm afraid of it."

The bishop chuckled and took him by the arm. "Young man, before we talk about seminary, let's learn how to ride the elevator!" And the seminary professor spent the next five minutes riding up and down the elevator with his prospective student, until the young man felt at home in it. More than a lesson in mechanics, Bill had learned a lesson in true greatness and kindness. Six years later, when Bishop Rudolph died, William Culbertson was asked to preach the memorial sermon at the council meeting of the New York and Philadelphia synod.

The seminary was founded in 1886 to prepare young men for the Reformed Episcopal ministry, and, in 1924, it was possible to enter the seminary directly after high school. It was not a large school; the faculty consisted of Bishop Rudolph, Dr. George Handy Wailes, and Bishop Robert Westly Peach. But size does not always determine force, and William Culbertson's seminary days had a lasting impact on his life, both academically and spiritually. In 1961, he wrote to his former professor, Dr. Wailes:

Almost daily there are those experiences which come to me that make me thank God for the three years I had in the Seminary in 1924-27. God used you in a very wonderful way to help my understanding of the Word and to give me the tools to continue my study.

Philadelphia, in those days, was a mecca for well-known preachers, and the eager student tried to hear all of them. In 1957, he told the congregation at British Keswick:

It was my privilege to sit under the ministry of dear servants of God from Great Britain who visited America when I was a boy and as I grew older and was in a theological seminary. One of those dear men of God was Dr. G. Campbell Morgan.

All his life, he was an admirer of Campbell Morgan; and his admiration for the great expositor created a bit of a problem when he was courting Catharine Gantz, because she preferred F. B. Meyer! Ultimately, they agreed that *both* men were good, and a truce was declared. During one of F. B. Meyer's visits to Philadelphia, he conducted a service "For Men Only," at which he dealt with the subject of personal purity. William Culbertson attended that service. After the message, an elderly man seated in front of him, turned to the young student, gripped his hand, and, with a trembling voice, said, "Young man, I wish I had heard that sermon when I was your age, *and had taken it to heart!*" To say the least, the effect was tremendous.

"I have forgotten much of what Dr. Meyer said that day," Dr. Culbertson stated in later years, "but I never forgot the face and the voice of that old man."

Never underestimate the influence of godly teachers. At British Keswick in 1954, Dr. Culbertson said, "I had a teacher who used a phrase which I have never been able to forget. One day he spoke about the 'consequences of *forgiven sin.*'"

This emphasis on practical holiness became the hallmark of his own ministry and the means of blessing and victory to thousands of Christians. In his last Founder's Week message, Dr. Culbertson mentioned another basic spiritual truth that came to him forcefully during his seminary days.

> One of my teachers in early days was speaking to me in his home in central Pennsylvania. As I was about to leave him, I had the temerity to ask him a question—not because I didn't know the answer, but because I wanted to hear it from his lips. I said, "My brother, you have often said you make it the practice of your life upon waking in the morning to first thank God that your body is the temple of the Spirit of God." "Yes, that's right." I said, "Why do you do that?" He replied, "My brother, first of all I want that truth to live. I want it to be vital and vibrant. I want it to be known and realized in my life every day that my body is a temple of the Spirit of God." "Yes," I said, "and what else?" He said so simply and yet so helpfully, "And second, it makes a difference in the way I live."

On Thursday evening, May 19, 1927, William Culbertson graduated from the Reformed Episcopal Seminary. There were three other students in the class: George W. Doherty, Howell S. Foster, and Howard G. Nyce. The commencement address was given by a professor of history from the University of Pennsylvania, Donald Grey Barnhouse. William Culbertson had set the sails of his life, and now his ministry would begin.

"God's purpose is that you and I, as His yielded servants, walking day by day in faith, shall know His enablement, His strengthening, and His life. Nothing less should make us willing to assume such a terrifying responsibility as a call to the ministry."

"Man To Man"
Recorded March 8, 1966

TWO

The Pastor

In January, 1927, while he was a senior at the seminary, William Culbertson was invited to preach at the Grace Reformed Episcopal Church in Collingdale, Pennsylvania, a suburb of Philadelphia. Bishop Rudolph recommended him to the vestry of the church as a young man "faithful to the Word of God, held in high regard by his professors, with a great potential as a minister." At that time, the Collingdale church was experiencing difficulties: fewer than fifty were attending the services, and about fifteen faithful souls were keeping the midweek prayer meeting going. There was a group in the church that saw nothing wrong with using bazaars and sales to finance the ministry, while a spiritual nucleus was beseeching God for a dedicated pastor who would strengthen and build the church.

The small congregation was deeply impressed with the message they heard, and the vestry invited the young preacher back for several Sundays. Finally, the vestry voted to extend him a call.

Dear Mr. Culbertson:

Confirming the verbal invitation to you, at a special meeting of the Wardens and Vestrymen of Grace Church held April 10th, to become Minister-in-Charge of Grace Church, after prayer for Divine leading it was by unanimous consent voted to extend to you an invitation to become Minister-in-Charge of Grace Church, Collingdale, effective as of Easter Sunday, April 17, 1927, with salary of $1800 per annum.

It has been the earnest prayer of the entire membership of the church as well as the Vestry that God would lead you to undertake His work in this field, where with consecrated leadership we believe much can be done to further His kingdom on earth.

Understanding your willingness to accept this invitation we pray that His richest blessing be upon you and your work in His service.

The new pastor soon discovered that the basic problem in the church was an ignorance of the deeper truths of the Word of God. Never one to sweep down upon a situation and change everything at once, William Culbertson patiently and prayerfully began to teach the Word of God in his own quiet and loving manner. He began to preach sermon series and to advertize them on cards that his members could distribute in the community. One such card announced a series of the "He is able" passages in the Bible, dealing with subjects such as salvation, deliverance, subjugation, preservation, and "the mystery of Israel." From the very beginning of his ministry, William Culbertson had an interest in prophecy in general and Israel in particular.

The Word of God did its work, as he knew it would. There was a slow but steady growth; people began to pray publicly who had never before participated in a prayer service; and the church leaders began to trust God to meet the needs of the ministry. They had been accustomed to raising the budget by means of church suppers and bazaars, but their pastor was convinced that these methods were not scriptural. "I think we should depend solely on the free-will offerings of the people," he told his vestrymen.

"Then you will not receive your salary!" they replied.

"I would like to suggest a venture of faith," he said. "Each month pay all the bills, making my salary the last payment. If any month there is insufficient money in the treasury, I will not be paid at all. In this way, I'm the only one to suffer; but I believe you will never lack sufficient funds."

How could they turn down such a fair proposal? They accepted it, and not once did their pastor go without his salary. At the end of the first year, the church had met all its obligations and there was a surplus, for the first time in years!

Former members still recall that his visits in the homes were "like a breath of fresh air." He could enter into family worship or family fun, and glorify God in both. He loved his people and tried to minister to them in every situation, and they grew under his ministry. He sought to win the lost to Christ; he searched out the careless church members and brought them back into the fold. It was not easy for a single young man, fresh out of seminary, to shepherd this flock, but he did so with amazing success; and his people knew that their pastor walked with God.

His ministry in Collingdale was noticed by other churches, including the Grace Reformed Episcopal Church of Havre de Grace, Maryland. The clerk of the vestry wrote him in October, 1927, asking if he would consider a call; and he replied,

> With regard to your communication, after prayerful consideration I believe the Lord still has much work for me to do in my present charge, so I therefore feel that I must forgo your gracious invitation to become minister-in-charge of your church. The work at Havre-de-Grace impressed me,

and I pray that the Lord will raise up a man for you that shall carry on the work of our Savior in the place that is so dear to your heart. Remember me kindly to the members in Havre-de-Grace.

"Dr. Culbertson excelled in letter writing," observes Harold Cook, a long-time member of the faculty at the Moody Bible Institute. "It was a gift." His method of answering his mail was not mysterious. He simply read each letter carefully, prayed about the matters involved, and sat down and wrote a longhand reply. This, he would consider further and revise as necessary. Then he would send out the final copy. In the above letter, he crossed out the sentence, "There is a feeling of regret that I cannot be in two places at one time." No doubt, when he read his first draft, that sentence impressed him as being a bit arrogant; and so he deleted it. It is safe to say that few, if any, letters received his signature if there was one word or sentence that might be misunderstood or possibly pain the reader.

In 1928, Pastor Culbertson began to teach at the Philadelphia School of the Bible, now known as the Philadelphia College of the Bible; and shortly after, he also took up teaching responsibilities at the Reformed Episcopal Seminary. It was no secret that teaching was his first love, particularly the teaching of Paul's epistles and Bible geography. The subject of Bible geography was almost a passion with him. In later years, if he found himself in a meeting where the speaker was somewhat less than challenging, he would sit and study the maps in the back of his Bible. In 1952, when Dr. Culbertson made the first of five visits to the Holy Land, someone asked him how he liked it, and he replied quietly, "Well, it's just as I expected it to be!"

The most important event of the Collingdale pastorate was his marriage on March 16, 1929, to Catharine Gantz. They had begun dating back in 1925, and on their sixth date, he had proposed! "So far as I know," she recalls, "that proposal was the only unpredictable thing he ever did, and I accepted on the spot!" She was living in nearby Aldan, Pennsylvania, which made it convenient for the busy pastor to visit her. The ceremony took place at the Aldan Union Church, and the pastor, William Allan Dean, officiated. Howard Criswell, one of the groom's old friends from Addison Henry days, served as an usher; and H. S. Foster, pastor of the Grace Reformed Episcopal Church of Schuylkill, was the best man.

It is worth noting that, during their dating days and the early months of their marriage, William and Catharine did not agree completely on everything. For one thing, she was Arminian in her beliefs, while he was Calvinistic. "He finally converted me!" she recalls. Then, they had some disagreement over baptism: she preferred immersion while he felt that the Scriptures taught pouring. Actually, all during his ministry, baptism was not an issue with him, and he practiced both sprinkling and immersion. They also disagreed about education: she favored the Bible school while he preferred the seminary. He had ample opportunity to study both, since he was teaching at the Reformed Episcopal Seminary and the Philadelphia School of the Bible; and it is significant that he invested most of his life as a teacher and administrator in a Bible institute. It is also significant that he helped to develop the kind of curriculum that made it possible for the institute graduate to go on for further education.

When they returned from their honeymoon in Washington D.C. and Baltimore, they set up housekeeping in a rented cottage at 924 Bedford Avenue, Collingdale. The first of their four children, Joy, was born during their Collingdale ministry, and they almost lost her. It had been a difficult delivery, and it was discovered that the baby was choking. God was merciful to the young parents and their firstborn;

the baby survived and lived up to her name as she brightened the home.

❊   ❊   ❊

For seven years, the church of St. John's-by-the-Sea, Ventnor, New Jersey, had been without a regular pastor. Located just two blocks from the Atlantic Ocean, the church was in a resort area and, consequently, enjoyed good crowds during the summer season. It was not too difficult to secure well-known preachers for the summer months, and it is likely that the regular congregation developed into accomplished "sermon tasters" who could make life difficult for any pastor they might call. Among the Reformed Episcopal clergy of that synod, there was a general agreement that nobody could suit them. William Culbertson himself made the remark, "I just wish they'd call me so I could refuse!"

They did call him. Two days after Joy was born, he received a special-delivery letter from the church vestry.

July 17, 1930

At a well-attended Business Meeting of the Church of Saint-John's-by-the-Sea, held last evening, a unanimous call was extended to you, to become the Rector of the church.

It was voted the salary we can offer you at this time is to be $3000.00 per year, which of course would be paid monthly, and the use of the Rectory, which will require some repairs.

It is our desire that the time of beginning your ministry with us should be October first, or a date that would be agreeable to you.

There has been much prayer, and it will continue that the Lord will lead you that you may be guided to a decision in this matter that will be prompted, honored and confirmed by the Holy Spirit, and that the wide open door at Ventnor may disclose to your own vision, opportunities for the abundant exercise of the gifts that the Lord has bestowed upon you.

It is not likely that Pastor Culbertson was greatly moved
by the complimentary contents of the letter, or by the offer
of an increased salary and the use of a rectory. In his usual
manner, he prayed, discussed the matter with his wife, and
sincerely sought the Lord's will. His first inclination was to
decline, but Catharine felt they should keep on praying. A
week later, he received a letter from his good friend and
former pastor, Harold S. Laird, who was preaching at St.
John's-by-the-Sea for the month of July and knew the church
rather well.

> First of all I want to congratulate you both on the arrival
> of the little girl. I heard the good news Sunday evening at
> church. We are all rejoicing with you in this which to our
> minds is the greatest blessing that can come to any man
> and wife. We trust and pray that Catharine is well and
> that the baby is fine, too. We can imagine the joy that fills
> the hearts of the grandparents, too, on both sides. Please
> congratulate them, too, for us.
>
> The other reason for my writing is to express to you my
> deep interest in the matter of the call that has been ex-
> tended to you from St. John's. I realize that you will be
> moved finally by just one thing in this matter and that is
> what you are led to believe to be the will of God. I am
> sure He will make His will clear to you.
>
> How happy I should be to see you here, if it be the
> Lord's will. For some time I have felt that this church
> must have an active pastor. When I think of what has been
> accomplished here without a regular pastor, I have great
> hopes for it under the leadership of the right man of God.
>
> I believe you would be wonderfully happy here in fel-
> lowship with the younger men who are now here. There is
> a fine fellow by the name of Fuller at the Chelsea Baptist
> Church, a recent graduate of Princeton Seminary and a
> Premillennial Fundamentalist. Then too there is a young
> fellow just graduated from Westminster Seminary at the

First Baptist Church. I am told there is developing a real spirit among the ministers here. They have secured a permit for open-air meetings on the beach, and are having some great meetings there.

The Lord does seem to have directed the hearts of these people toward you. We shall continue earnestly in prayer for His clear guidance in this important matter. He will guide you as definitely as He has guided me and I can say that I have never been in doubt about being in His will.

The rough draft of Pastor Culbertson's reply to the church was written on the back of the envelope in which their letter arrived!

Although we have been much in prayer, the Lord has not yet made clear His will. Realizing the importance of the step, I'm sure you will understand my hesitancy.

Would it be possible for me to meet the Vestry some evening of the week of the 24th? There are a few matters that I would like to talk to you about, for I believe they would make clear what step should be taken. I would appreciate it if the meeting could be arranged for the early evening so that I might get back to Collingdale that night.

He began his ministry at St. John's-by-the-Sea on Wednesday, October 1. He and Catharine and the baby lived in an apartment for six weeks while the church made necessary repairs on the rectory, which was located right next to the church building. On Friday evening, October 17, William Culbertson was officially installed as rector, with his friend Harold S. Laird bringing the address. He ministered in Ventnor only two and a half years, but they were happy years both for him and the church. Of course, when a church has been without a pastor for many years, there is a tendency for certain people to take over various programs of the church, and the arrival of a leader is a challenge to their authority. One officer in particular was especially dictatorial and tried to take advantage of the youthful new pastor; but in the end, the pastor's patience—and prayers—won out.

Before long, the little cards announcing sermon series began to appear. One card carries this statement above the list of sermon topics: "In response to several requests the Pastor will preach a series of sermons on subjects related to the return of Christ." Some of the topics were: "The Church at Christ's Appearing," "Israel at Christ's Revelation," "The Gentile Nations at Christ's Revelation," and "The Destiny of the Unrighteous." At the bottom of the card, the pastor quoted Matthew 24:44, "Therefore be ye also ready: for in such an hour as *ye think not* the Son of man cometh." The italicized words indicated his belief in the imminent return of Christ.

An item in one of the church bulletins reveals his continued concern for Israel: "Friends of the Jewish Work are invited to their Friday evening meeting at 8 o'clock. The meeting is held in the mission, 2603 Pacific Avenue. There is a real need for people to attend this service so as to make it as attractive to the Hebrew as possible." He often invited those involved in Jewish evangelism to speak at the church's midweek service. The church bulletin indicates that the pastor had a full schedule of meetings each month, and the growth of the church revealed that he was faithful to his calling.

Another ministry that attracted him was the Atlantic City Bible School, an evening school that met in the YWCA. One evening, a local pastor was introducing him and thought he would take advantage of the speaker's denominational affiliation and inject a little humor. "This is the Reverend William Culbertson," the pastor said, "a deformed and unformed Episcopalian." After the laughter subsided, the speaker quietly replied: "I am neither deformed or unformed, but informed, and *transformed by God's grace!*" In later years, very few people dared to jest publicly with Dr. Culbertson, but if they did, he was usually able to lift the meeting to a higher spiritual level by his own careful response.

While the Reformed Episcopal Church was his ecclesiastical home, William Culbertson always enjoyed the fellowship of believers from many denominations. During his nearly three years at Ventnor, he especially enjoyed being with David Otis Fuller, who pastored the Chelsea Baptist Church; Carl MacIntire, who was at the Presbyterian church in Chelsea; and Harold Commons, pastor of the Baptist church in Atlantic City. They not only had great times together, as only pastors can, but they shared a common burden for reaching the lost. That whole area was a vast harvest field during the vacation months, and the men held regular open-air meetings on the beach. "That was the hardest preaching I ever did," Dr. Culbertson recalled in later years. "If we had an ocean breeze, it was so noisy nobody could hear you. But if we had a land breeze, you ate mosquitoes!"

He also continued his teaching ministry at the Reformed Episcopal Seminary and the Philadelphia School of the Bible. He recalled those years in a message given at British Keswick in 1957.

> Once a week it was my duty to go to Philadelphia, a distance of some sixty or seventy miles from Ventnor. I had the privilege of teaching in two schools in Philadelphia, one in the morning and the other in the evening, just to keep out of mischief! And I recall riding the train to go up to teach, very early in the morning; and the time of the year that I love to think about was the spring, because the railroad tracks went right through so many of the beautiful orchards of New Jersey. . . . My, they were magnificent, those pink blossoms and that green of the grass! There is nothing like spring grass, you know; oh, it is beautiful. And I had been looking at it all, trying to take it in. Sud-

denly, I would remember, it is all going to die. Before ever there is a bit of fruit, it must all die. And, my friend, before there is ever any fruit of the Spirit, you have to die. For, fruit is borne, not by doing, but by dying.

Dying to self was a truth that William Culbertson not only believed and taught, but also practiced; and during the spring of 1933, he was going to have a new opportunity to discover its power again.

❋   ❋   ❋

"If you don't come, the church will be closed by August; and if you do come, it might close anyway!"

The church referred to was the Reformed Episcopal Church of the Atonement, located in the Germantown section of Philadelphia. It was not that the church had received no spiritual guidance; D. M. Stearns, the well-known Bible teacher, had once pastored there and had faithfully taught the Word. Nor was there any lack of dedicated lay leadership; the Philip Howard, Jr., family were members there, and Mr. Howard was a vestryman. (The daughter, Betty, would one day go to the mission field with her husband, Jim Elliot.) The problem was that a previous pastor had gone "high church" and had precipitated a division in the congregation. It was the kind of situation for which William Culbertson was ideally prepared; or, as his wife later reflected, "Every place we went, it was a *necessity!*"

But they would pay a price. The Germantown congregation could guarantee no salary, and they owned no rectory. The Culbertsons were very happy in Ventnor, and God was blessing the ministry. Little Joy now had a baby brother, William Robert, born January 18, 1933; and taking two little children into a new and difficult situation would demand a great deal of faith.

He preached at the church early that spring and received

an official call on March 30. By April 10, the Culbertsons knew that it was God's will for them to accept, and this they communicated to the vestry. The rector's warden at Germantown was Philip E. Howard, Jr., who sent the following reply:

> It was with deep gratitude to God that the members of the Vestry heard read last evening your letter of April 10, accepting their call to you to become Rector of the Church of the Atonement. We are also glad to know that you will be with us the first week in May. We presume this means that you will conduct the services on Sunday, May 7, and the regular services thereafter.
>
> Since the invitation was extended to you, the Vestry and many members of the Church have been earnestly praying that God would lead you to accept, and as you have also sought the Lord's mind in the matter and have felt led to come, we believe that His will is being done and are deeply thankful for His guidance. We look confidently to our Heavenly Father to bless you richly in your ministry here, and to make of the Church a strong and united witness for His Name.

The official installation was held on Sunday evening, May 21, with Bishop Robert W. Peach officiating. Bishop Peach had been one of William Culbertson's instructors at the seminary. The Culbertsons rented a house for two years until the church was able to purchase its own rectory. The new pastor started right in teaching and preaching the Word of God in his own quiet, loving way; and before long, the church was united and moving ahead in its ministry.

The pastor accepted the responsibility of teaching the men's Bible class, and soon had them involved in witnessing and soul-winning. The men led the services at various rescue missions and also shared Christ in their daily occupations. At least one of the men in the class developed into a gifted soul-winner, and later became the pastor of an independent church. As in his previous churches, Pastor Culbertson preached sermon series and distributed invitation cards. One such card announces a series on "the mysteries of the Bible," nine messages dealing with the mystery of the kingdom, the rapture, the olive tree, and others. During his nine years at the Church of the Atonement, William Culbertson expounded many entire books of the Bible, including the gospel of John, The Revelation, Job, Daniel, and (his final series as pastor) the book of Ecclesiastes.

Very wisely, the officers of the church permitted their new pastor to continue teaching and also to share in a wider ministry as a Bible conference speaker, for which he was already in great demand. Because of this heavy schedule, he was excused from the routine visitation work that he would gladly have fulfilled had he been able; but he was always on hand when any of his people were in special need. When he was absent from his pulpit, he arranged for one of his friends to preach, always an outstanding man of God. The church was privileged to hear such men as William Pettingill, Frank Gaebelein, L. Sale-Harrison, Tom Rees, Lewis Sperry Chafer, Harold Commons, and E. Schuyler English.

The vestry also encouraged their pastor to complete his college studies; so in 1936, he enrolled in the teacher's college at Temple University in Philadelphia, receiving his degree in 1939. That same year, his seminary granted him an honorary doctor of divinity degree. Several of his themes, written for his college English course, reveal his ability to analyze a subject, evaluate it, and make a practical application for life. Some of his topics were: "Swift as a Satirist," "The Man Whitman in His Poetry," "My Favorite Portion of the Bible: Psalm Twenty-Nine," and a review of *Huckleberry Finn.* His comments on Psalm 29 are worth quoting:

I have chosen the 29th Psalm—the Psalm of the Thunder

Storm—as my favorite portion of the Bible, though I must confess that passages from Isaiah, John, and Paul vie with the Psalm. But the exquisiteness of form, the splendidness of imagination, and the loftiness of sentiment have attracted me to the Psalm. I shall develop three reasons for my choice of this Psalm: (1) the graphic description of the storm; (2) the literary merit of its form; and (3) the vicarious experience of life which it affords.

In the paper, he shows a good understanding of the forms of Hebrew poetry as well as the beauty of the English translation. His closing paragraph reveals clearly that the writer is a preacher of the Word!

I can only say that I believe it was a stroke of genius which caused the Psalmist to conclude the Psalm with the word *peace*. You know the peace, the quiet, the untrammeled serenity of earth after the storm. Beethoven has beautifully presented the after-calm in his Pastoral Symphony. You know that tranquillity in nature. Have you never known the same ecstatic experience after the storm and stress of trouble? I have.

Professor Ferguson's comment at the close of the paper was, "Very slow warming up, but excellent toward the end."

It was while he was pastoring the Church of the Atonement that William Culbertson was made a bishop of the Reformed Episcopal Church, an office that he held for the rest of his life.

> *"In conscience before God we search
> the Scriptures to find that church which
> to us most nearly approximates the truth
> as it is in Jesus, and we give that church
> our love, our devotion, our loyalty, for
> His sake."*
>
> Address to the council
> The Reformed Episcopal Church, 1950

THREE

The Bishop

"Now don't go getting yourself elected bishop!"

Those were Catharine's parting words to her husband as he left for the meeting of the New York and Philadelphia synod that bright day in April, 1937. Actually, he was sure somebody else would be elected anyway, and that her warning was rather unnecessary. For one thing, he was young; the minimum age for a bishop was thirty, and he was only thirty-one. And he was very busy as a pastor, teacher, and conference speaker, and really would have no time for the duties of the bishop.

Two different candidates were presented to the council, but neither of them could command the required two-thirds majority vote. A group of men approached William Culbertson privately and asked him if he would be willing to serve. His reply was typical:

"I covet no offices, but if the synod feels I can help to keep our church true to its articles of faith, I will accept it as the will of God." Then he added a significant postscript: "I want it understood that if I'm called to another field of work, and I go, that you won't think I've let you down." One is tempted to believe that already God was preparing him for a much wider ministry and that he knew it.

His name was presented, and the inevitable happened: he was elected by a unanimous vote. Up to that time, the only unanimous election had been when the Reformed Episcopal Church was founded and the first bishop elected! The young bishop-elect telephoned his wife and gave her the news in a rather nonchalant manner, an action he was to repeat years later when elected president of the Moody Bible Institute.

The consecration service was held Friday, April 30, 1937, at the Church of the Atonement, with Dr. George Handy Wailes bringing the sermon. The prayer for the bishop-elect was give by Edwin A. Bustard, who also pastored at Collingdale and became a lifelong friend of the Culbertsons.

Bishop Culbertson's responsibilities involved supervising the churches in eastern New York and Pennsylvania, New Jersey, Maryland, and Delaware. This meant visiting each church at least once a year, giving spiritual counsel to the pastors, and exercising oversight in the total ministry of the synod. Add to these demands his pastoral work, his teaching ministry, and his wider preaching ministry, and you can see that the young bishop had quite a calling to fulfill! Bishop Howard Higgins graciously gave assistance with synodical responsibilities so that Bishop Culbertson was not attempting the impossible; but his new office did require him to be away from his own pulpit more frequently. But his congregation said of him, as did Campbell Morgan's congregation in London, "We would rather have our pastor half the time than any other pastor all the time!"

It is interesting to consider some of the matters that came to his desk because he was a bishop. A pastor wrote that he was concerned about the seeming "dead orthodoxy" of the denomination (and what group has not faced this charge?), and he wondered if he should seek another denomination. "Frankly," the pastor went on, "I feel that our leadership has become habituated to smallness and that vision is lacking. I know that we are orthodox, but sometimes I wonder whether lifeless orthodoxy is much more pleasing to the Lord than active liberalism."

Bishop Culbertson replied:

> Of course, from a personal standpoint, I very much hope that you will not see any necessity of withdrawing from the Reformed Episcopal Church. While it is true that there are certain weaknesses so far as vision and virile accomplishments are concerned, on the other hand, the withdrawal of a man like yourself would mean a further weakening of the denomination.

> My own feeling with regard to the Reformed Episcopal Church is that I am happy to be in fellowship with a group which insists so definitely upon the solid truths of the Word of God.

In his 1950 address to the council of the Reformed Episcopal Church, he underscored the importance of the church's ministering to the needs of people today.

> I'm going to suggest that, in order to speak to our own generation, we must: *First,* make our doctrinal standards live; *second,* we must have a renewed and quickened sense of the church; and, *third,* we must know a deeper and fuller consecration and evangelistic zeal.

> We pride ourselves, and rightly, upon the fact that we can recite the Apostle's Creed and the Nicene Creed, in common with Christians through the centuries of the church. We count it a distinct privilege to be able to give our Amen to the Thirty-five Articles of Religion adopted by our founders. . . . But what do these standards mean to us

and to the man on the street? In order to make our doctrinal standards live, I think first of all we must translate them into a language that man of this generation can understand. . . . Quote the Scriptures, quote the doctrinal statement, but let us rid ourselves of the old cliches of human manufacture and get where the people are. . . . But there is something more than the translation of our doctrinal standards into language which can be understood by the average man. There is also the translation of our doctrinal standards into the very life that we live.

Obviously, the needs mentioned in this address are not peculiar to any one denomination. Bishop Culbertson loved his church and defended it and sought to strengthen and extend its ministry; but he was not blind to the needs of his church or, for that matter, of Christians everywhere. He was a devoted foe of "easy Christianity." In his Founder's Week message of 1958, he exclaimed, "Every once in a while I have to stop and say, 'Culbertson, what are you living for? How much is it costing you to be a disciple of the Lord?'" He would not ask others to pay a price that he himself was unwilling to pay.

He accepted the office of bishop with the understanding that he would defend the doctrines of the faith. He was always fearful lest the Reformed Episcopal Church compromise its convictions and go the way of other once evangelical denominations. He was not a crusader in the sense that Spurgeon meant when he talked about preachers who "walk around with a revolver in their pocket." In that same 1958 Founder's Week message, he openly differed with those who substitute "vehemency in defense of the faith for vitality in living the faith." But he was not one to hide when there was an enemy in the field, nor was he one to shun the use of the word *fundamentalist*. In his 1966 Founder's Week message, he declared: "And as president of Moody Bible Institute, I want to sound again the word of warning. If we as orthodox, as Evangelicals, as fundamentalists move from this doctrine [the inspiration of the Word of God] we are doomed to disaster." Perhaps his attitude was best revealed by a statement in his 1955 Founder's Week message:

> Surely the Lord's servant is not to strive, but to be gentle toward all. God help us to be that, and not to enter a fight simply for the sake of a fight; not to go around with a chip on our shoulder waiting for somebody to push it off so we can slug him! But do not confuse gentleness with lack of conviction. Do not make the mistake of saying the Bible teaches that Christians should be spineless and like jelly-fish, a sort of Mr. Milquetoast, convictionless. The Bible nowhere presents any such picture of the child of God.

Even after he became president of the Institute, he continued to exercise spiritual oversight in his denomination and regularly reported his activities to the presiding bishop. He often assisted in confirmation services and carefully tried to determine that the candidates had truly been born again and were not merely going through a religious routine. One confirmation service led to an interesting letter from one of the candidates, written six years after the event. Apparently, confirmation had not been a vital spiritual experience for her because she had never been converted; but when the bishop had asked her personally, "Do you confess and declare that Jesus Christ, the Son of God, is your Lord and Saviour?" she had answered "I do," as though she had been born again. Every pastor has had this experience, if not with a confirmation class, at least with baptismal candidates or applicants for church membership. In her long letter to Bishop Culbertson, the young lady, now seventeen, took him to task for not being sure she was really saved; because now, six years later, she had truly been born again. "I was shocked when I learned that you are the president of Moody

Bible Institute and that you confirmed me when I was yet unsaved. But I am so thankful that God's great mercy allowed me to come in contact with those who are truly His children."

Bishop Culbertson's reply ignored the innuendos in the young lady's letter ("After I was saved, I was really baptized the way Jesus wants us to be"), and graciously answered her questions.

> I think that every true pastor devoutly desires that each one who unites with the church be a true believer and an earnest follower of the Lord. He must do all in his power to guarantee such a result. But, alas, what one of us dares to claim that it is so. Pastors and boards can and have been deceived. Sometimes even otherwise faithful pastors fail to make the message plain. In any case, the Lord will not fail. You are a witness to that, and I am glad that your present affiliation has met your need. . . . And, so far as immersion is concerned, it may be administered in the Reformed Episcopal Church at the request of the candidate. I myself have so administered it.

> Let me answer you that I know of hundreds of Reformed Episcopalians who know what it is to be born again. It just may be that your statement, "I guess I never really paid attention to what was being said," is at point in the matter. . . . In the service itself, I addressed several questions to the confirmees. You answered "I do" to my question: "Do you confess and declare that Jesus Christ, the Son of God, is your Lord and Saviour?"

> Thank the Lord for your present experience. God bless you and use you in it.

William Culbertson was a firm believer and promoter of true biblical ecumenicity, but not fellowship with those who deny the faith. On New Year's Day, 1939, he preached a message at the Church of the Atonement on the subject,

"Separation—True and False." His text was 2 Corinthians 6:17, "Wherefore Come ye out from among them, and be ye separate, saith the Lord, And touch no unclean thing; And I will receive you" (ASV). He pointed out several kinds of false separation, that of the Pharisees, for example, or the monastic groups. "There is schismatic separation," he said, "when our notions separate us from true believers, when we separate ourselves unto men or mere opinions. There is no cause for separation when men differ in minor details but not in the great doctrines of Scripture."

Then he defined true separation: it is when God makes a difference (Ex 11:7, "That ye may know how that Jehovah doth make a distinction between the Egyptians and Israel," ASV). "When God demands separation, He is asking that we work out in experience what He has already wrought in fact." He then applied this principle to marriage, fraternal and social fellowship, and church membership. He closed the sermon with an enunciation of the positive principle that true separation is "unto God and unto a life of holiness."

Because of this deep-seated conviction, William Culbertson would not endorse the National Council of Churches or the World Council of Churches, or any of their agencies. He did not break fellowship with pastors whose churches were in denominations that belonged to these groups, but he was careful that everyone knew where he stood. When a world-famous ecumenical leader crusaded across the country for a "federal union of Christians," Dr. Culbertson exposed the error of this program in an editorial in *Moody Monthly*.

> The Word of God is clear that there will be ecclesiastical union in the end-time (*vide* Revelation 17 and 18), but what union!
>
> Not without reason have evangelicals stressed unity rather

than union. But you may have a unity of one of two kinds: a unity of disbelief or a unity of belief. The so-called modernists are not much concerned about beliefs; they can have unity with a minimum of requirements. However, on closer inspection, it will be evident that this unity is one of indifference rather than conviction. On the other hand, you may have a unity of true believers in the Word of God. This unity is organic and divine, not institutional and human.

We are not for selfish, petty denominational competition. We believe in the unity of believers in Christ. We thank God for organizations which go beyond denominational lines in the sense that all evangelicals can co-operate in them—without sacrificing any fundamentals of the faith. However, we cannot be a part of any movement which does not insist on the supremacy of God's Living Word and God's Written Word.

When he discovered that the rector of a Reformed Episcopal Church had participated in an interfaith "Christian unity" service, he immediately wrote him a letter of protest and warning.

For me, the Word of God is clear on the question of the position of our Lord. Whether it be a liberal Protestant or anyone else who denies the deity of Christ, I must not participate in even possible affront to my Lord. John 5:23; 14:6; Acts 4:12; I John 5:11, 12 are clear.

Unless there is something more than I can see in the newspaper item referred to above, I have no alternative than to ask that my name be no longer connected in even tenuous fashion with———Church, and that I must let the presiding Bishop know that I no longer will be available for episcopal visitation to the church.

You know that it pains me so to write. I have no question concerning your love for the Lord and I love you and your

> people. But my allegiance to the Lord Jesus Christ must come first—and I cannot allow my name to be associated in an ecumenical movement that includes those who deny Him. This difference and other differences are far too great to give the impression that we can forget them in favor of ecumenicity.

In this particular case, the matter was straightened out to the satisfaction of the pastor, Bishop Culbertson, and the presiding bishop, Howard Higgins.

In writing to Bishop Higgins about another church matter (a proposed revision of the prayer book), Dr. Culbertson closed his letter with a paragraph that beautifully summarized his attitude about disagreements in the church:

> May the Lord lead us aright. We must be concerned about the peace as well as the purity of the Church. It is distressing to see good men troubled of conscience about a question that probably could be settled without great loss liturgically or otherwise.

He was not one to sacrifice purity for peace, but neither was he one to declare war over a matter that could be handled in better fashion. His good friend, Dr. Robert K. Rudolph, son of Bishop Rudolph, put it this way: "I always found him a true realist. He never allowed his devotion to the ideals which the Lord set before us to blind him to 'the reals' which the Christian must face in dealing with sinful men."

"A bishop then must be blameless," Paul wrote to Timothy; and all who knew Bishop Culbertson well would agree that he qualified.

"There is hardship to be faced. The Lord doesn't give us easy tasks normally. Sometimes He asks us to do things that we ourselves would not choose to do, and therefore we find them difficult."

Chapel address
September 28, 1970

FOUR

The Move to Chicago

On November 1, 1934, Dr. Will H. Houghton became the fourth president of the Moody Bible Institute, succeeding Dr. James M. Gray who had devoted thirty years of his life to "the school that D. L. Moody founded." Dr. Gray himself had urged the trustees to call the energetic, godly pastor of New York City's Calvary Baptist Church, and the counsel of other men of God confirmed his choice. When the trustees asked Dr. H. A. Ironside, then pastor of the Moody Church in Chicago, for his suggestions, he gave them two names, Will H. Houghton and a pastor in Texas. When he was asked what was so special about Will H. Houghton, Dr. Ironside replied, "He won't be afraid to surround himself with men who may be bigger than himself!" One of the men Will Houghton "captured" for the Moody Bible Institute was William Culbertson, and it took three years to do it.

It is likely that Wilbur M. Smith first called Dr. Houghton's attention to the pastor of the Church of the Atonement;

and whenever Dr. Houghton was in Philadelphia and was free from a preaching engagement, he went to hear the young bishop preach. He liked what he heard, and made up his mind that, if it was in God's will, William Culbertson would be a member of his faculty. The fact that Dr. Culbertson was a bishop in the Reformed Episcopal Church was very much in his favor; for Dr. James M. Gray had been rector of the First Reformed Episcopal Church of Boston and had taught English Bible at their seminary in Philadelphia.

Dr. Houghton invited Bishop Culbertson to speak at the 1939 Founder's Week conference, the first of many messages he would deliver at that conference in years to come. He spoke from Isaiah 53:4; his theme was "Smitten of God." His message shows careful study of the original Hebrew of Isaiah 53. It also shows a clear conviction about the substitutionary death of Christ on the cross. The address was printed in the April issue of *Moody Monthly*.

The long correspondence begins with a letter from Dr. Houghton dated May 9, 1939.

> For some months now you have been on my mind in regard to the matter about which I am going to write. It seems to me you have gifts and abilities which would make you valuable to this institution. Naturally I haven't any idea as to your own thought of your future. It may be that you consider the pastorate to be your field, but I wonder if in a work such as this there isn't an opportunity for you to multiply your life and influence. When I see the stream of young people going in and out of these doors, and realize the need the world has today of just what we are giving these youth, it seems to me that the investment of life here means more than it would anywhere else on the globe.
>
> Would you consider an invitation to the Faculty of the Moody Bible Institute? I believe you have teaching gifts and inclinations. Am I not right in this appraisal? There

would also be some opportunity to serve in Bible Conferences.

After discussing the general situation spiritually and financially at the Institute, Dr. Houghton closed with the kind of a personal challenge that was typical of his spiritual vision and vitality.

> The hand of God has very evidently been upon the Institute. There isn't any inclination here to take it out of His hand. We cannot help but believe that all of the past is but preparation for the significant hour in which we now stand. If we can but be true to the Word of God, and will yield ourselves to the fulness of the Holy Spirit's power, and diligently prepare all of the young people possible to carry the Gospel to the ends of the earth, only God knows what the future holds. With Modernism as dead as ever ("by this time . . . stinketh"), with the worldly churches dying of dry rot, and with so much of Fundamentalism impotent through various causes, there is surely a place of tremendous need for an institution of integrity, loyalty, faith, and power. May God make the Moody Bible Institute that kind of an institution!
>
> I know you will pray about this, and some of us are praying here. We want the will of the Lord in this, as in all things.

The next step was a personal conversation between the two men concerning the invitation. Dr. Houghton visited the Culbertsons at their home while he was ministering in the Philadelphia area, and this visit led to the following letter from Dr. Culbertson, dated June 8:

> This letter is to supplement our recent conversation concerning the gracious invitation to consider teaching at the Moody Bible Institute. I count that invitation one of the choicest opportunities ever offered me. While I know that

the work of the Moody Bible Institute surpasses an out-
sider's expectations, nevertheless I realize to some extent
the tremendous opportunities and possibilities which such
a work offers. My unwillingness to accept immediately is
in no way to be construed as a lack of interest or as ignorance of the wonderful field of service. But, as I said to
you when you were here, I find myself pretty much bound
in by present circumstances. While I am not so conceited
as to think that the work of the Reformed Episcopal
Church will go to ruin without me, nevertheless the Lord
so definitely put responsibility upon me that I believe I
would be untrue to His trust were I to leave now. As I
told you, there are several rather important matters before
the Church at this time. And since I have the confidence
of some of our fine Bible teaching young men, I do not
feel that I should desert the ship, until these items have
been cared for. In the meanwhile, in accordance with
your suggestion, Mrs. Culbertson and I shall be praying
for the Lord's will. And if that will should lead to Moody,
we shall be happy to respond; for we only want the will of
the Lord.

Two weeks later, the bishop received this reply:

I have your letter concerning the matter of your own possible connection with the Institute. While I accept the letter and your statement, I am not for a single moment giving up the idea, and I trust that one of these days the Lord
may lead you this way.

To add to the excitement of those days, their third child,
Paul, was born on July 29. During those busy days of caring
for the children, and serving as a busy pastor's wife, Catharine prayed much for the Lord's definite direction. She
loved the pastorate, and she was jealous over her husband's
gifts lest they be swallowed up by administrative duties,
something that could happen if they were to move to the

Institute. Along with her husband, she was greatly concerned about the strengthening of their denomination. For one thing, the church council in 1942 would be considering the issues of church union and possible association in the Federal Council of Churches, something that Dr. Culbertson would definitely oppose. Another problem was the naming of a successor, should he resign.

But the Institute benefited from Dr. Culbertson's spiritual ministry, for he was privileged to speak at the 1940 Founder's Week Conference. This time, he spoke on one of his favorite themes, the return of Christ for His church. His text was Song of Solomon 2:8-14, and his topic was "Christ's Message at His Coming." Interestingly, this was the same text and theme he used at the 1971 conference of the American Association for Jewish Evangelism, held at Winona Lake, Indiana. No one knew it then, but it was to be the last sermon he would ever preach in public. The sermon delivered in 1940 shows an amazing depth of understanding. The thirty-four-year-old bishop might have been youthful, but he was not immature.

Almost a year passed before Dr. Houghton sent the official call in a letter dated September 18, 1940.

Yesterday afternoon the Executive Committee met, and voted unanimously to extend to you a call to become a member of our Faculty, at a time convenient to yourself.

As to the time of starting your work with us, probably both of us have in mind September, 1941. However, if you found you could begin with us in the April term, we would be glad for that.

Now, my dear friend, I am sure you know that there is something more than a cold, formal call in this letter. The conviction has been with me for a long time that there is a place of high service for you in this school. That conviction has deepened as time has gone on, and there is real joy in my own heart in writing you of the action of the Executive Committee. I hope you and your good lady, as you pray together concerning this, may feel it to be the will of the Lord, and I hope it may mean many happy years of service together as our Lord tarries.

His closing paragraph was more prophetic than he realized at the time.

I cannot help but feel this is an important hour in the life of the Institute and in my own life, as I write this letter. In Day and Evening School at this moment we have nearly 2,500. Just think of it, man! Your young life, with many years ahead in the providence of God, and the opportunity of investing it, yes, multiplying it, in the hundreds and hundreds and hundreds of eager young people God will send here. I can't feel anything else than that He wants you here, but that is for you to decide. Please be sure of our sympathetic prayer and understanding in the days ahead as you think and pray this through, and be sure of our joy in some word from you when you are ready.

A paragraph like that would have compelled a lesser man to telegraph, "Coming immediately!" But not Bishop Culbertson. Too long he had practiced waiting on the Lord until the guidance needed was provided, and he was not now going to abandon his practice. "While we cannot say that the answer had come in finality," he wrote Dr. Houghton on October 25, "yet there are indications of the leading of the Lord. Just as soon as that conviction deepens, we shall let you know." Dr. Houghton must have read into that statement an acceptance of the call, because he was deeply grieved when on November 8, Dr. Culbertson wrote saying that he would not be coming.

Mrs. Culbertson and I believe that we know the will of the Lord concerning the gracious invitation of the Executive

Committee. We have, of course, spoken at length about the matter, but during the course of the last week we have arrived (almost simultaneously) at the same answer without any attempted collaboration. The particular basis upon which our judgment was founded—as nearly as one may analyze the formation of a conviction—was different for each of us, but the conclusion is the same. I find that, as much as I am personally attracted to the Institute, I cannot be free of conscience to accept now.

He goes on to explain the importance of the council confirming his successor, an event that could not take place until May, 1942. And since one of the men involved in the "old controversy," when he was elected bishop, would be involved, he would not like his resignation beforehand to open old wounds and resurrect buried problems.

I can assure you this decision costs me greatly, for teaching at Moody is not lightly esteemed by me. Furthermore, I recognize that whatever gift I have, it is largely in the teaching field—a field for which the episcopate is unlikely to offer much opportunity. However, I must leave such matters with the Lord.

This step is taken with the full realization that such an offer is not likely to be extended again. I recognize that the need of the Institute is such that the whole program cannot wait upon one man. And I can assure you that these considerations have not made any easier my ultimate decision. The open door, the abundant opportunity, the particular gift which in measure has been given me, full sympathy with the doctrinal statement and the Institute's standards of life, and the possible close fellowship with friends whom I greatly admire and trust—all these have argued clearly for another course. I can only repeat Luther's words: "Here I stand; I can do naught else." Believing that we know His will, we shall be content. We understand that He is able to rule and overrule.

For once, Dr. Houghton ran out of superlatives; but one can sense the warmth of his love in his reply dated November 18.

> To say I am disappointed is to put it mildly. However, I am not at all disposed to argue the matter with you, for you and your lady know the leading of the Lord. . . . While I accept your answer for the present, I do not feel that that necessarily closes the matter for the entire future. If you can see anything that would encourage me to reopen the discussion, please as a good friend frankly tell me. Neither of us wants anything that is out of the will of the Lord, and we can deal with each other in brotherly fashion concerning this, without any possibility of misunderstanding.

To add to the excitement of that 1940 Christmas season, the Culbertsons welcomed their fourth child, Ruth Catharine, who was born on December 1. But as far as the Institute invitation was concerned, matters seemed to quiet down. Dr. Culbertson spoke at the 1941 Founder's Week Conference on the subject "Why Saints Suffer." A few weeks later, on March 26, he received an urgent telegram from Dr. Houghton, and the matter was opened again:

> COULD YOU MEET ME TUESDAY, APRIL FIRST AT 10:00 AM BENJAMIN FRANKLIN HOTEL, PHILADELPHIA, FOR AN HOUR'S CONFERENCE? PLEASE WIRE COLLECT.

Dr. Culbertson wired that he would meet him, and he did. The conversation, of course, had to do with going to the Institute, but now a new factor was introduced: Dr. Culbertson would come as dean of education and not merely as another instructor. It seemed to the Culbertsons that the Lord's time had come, and the bishop wired Dr. Houghton on April 3:

> YES FOR THE FALL OF 1942 THE LORD WILLING.

Back came the president's reply:

> Praise the Lord for the good news in your wire. We will pray and plan along the line indicated in our conversation, and will hope for the consummation of the whole matter in due time.

Dr. P. B. Fitzwater, a veteran Institute teacher, was serving as acting dean, and Dr. Houghton wrote his dean-elect that Fitzwater "will surrender the responsibility at any moment. I am not writing this to urge you to come sooner than planned, but only frankly to state the case and tell you you will be welcome at any time."

Since 1939, Dr. Culbertson had spoken each year at Founder's Week, but the 1942 experience was different from the others. For one thing, in spite of precautions, the rumor leaked out that Bishop Culbertson would be coming on the faculty in the fall. After hearing his moving message on "The Bleating of the Sheep," the faculty and staff were all hoping the rumor was true! One staff member in particular, Miss May Hogan, was especially interested in Dr. Culbertson's future, since she had been the secretary in the dean's office since 1940, working first with Dr. Harold Lundquist, who resigned in 1941, and then with Dr. Fitzwater. If Dr. Culbertson was to be the new dean, then he would be her boss.

While the Culbertsons were in Chicago for the conference, they made a quick visit to several sections of the city with a view to finding a house. Anyone who has visited Chicago in February knows that the weather is usually very cold, snowy, and windy. "I think your idea of looking around to get a glimpse of various sections of the city is good," Dr. Houghton wrote him on January 6. "Of course, you must warn your lady not to interpret Chicago in the language of February! Even Germantown doesn't look so good some March days!" Also during the conference, the Culbertsons were shown around the Institute buildings by H. Coleman Crowell, who later became a close friend. They also lunched with Thomas S. Smith, father of faculty member Wilbur M. Smith, and a valued trustee of the Institute.

Dr. Houghton wanted to announce Dr. Culbertson's appointment in the July issue of *Moody Monthly*, the official Institute publication; but this meant letting the secret out at least two months before. The issue would come off the press on June 20; the bishop had planned to resign from the standing committee of the synod on June 9 and from the church on June 10, so the timing was perfect. On May 22, in Charleston, South Carolina, the general council of the Reformed Episcopal Church had approved the election of Bishop Higgins, so the stage was set for the big change. But all did not go as planned. The following telegrams tell the story.

JUNE 10, 1942

DR. WILL H. HOUGHTON
MIAMI BEACH, FLORIDA
TRIBUNE AND ASSOCIATED PRESS QUERIED TODAY ABOUT CULBERTSON. NEWS LEAKED IN EAST BECAUSE OF RESIGNATION. TRIED TO HOLD OFF GIVING STATEMENT UNTIL YOUR RETURN. DO YOU WANT TO WIRE ANNOUNCEMENT FOR PAPERS AND INSTITUTE FAMILY? WHAT ABOUT SUNDAY MORNING BROADCAST?

H. C. CROWELL

JUNE 11, 1942

RESIGNATIONS MADE AND ACCEPTED. READY TO BEGIN IN SEPTEMBER. REGRET THAT CIRCUMSTANCES BEYOND MY CONTROL LET NEWS OUT TO PAPERS IN PHILADELPHIA. TRUST THAT WHATEVER ANNOUNCEMENT YOU WISH TO

MAKE IN CHICAGO WILL NOT BE AFFECTED.
MAY THE LORD LEAD AND BLESS.

WM. CULBERTSON

JUNE 11, 1942

H. C. CROWELL
153 INSTITUTE PLACE
YES RELEASE NEWS. "ON BEHALF OF THE BOARD
OF TRUSTEES THE PRESIDENT ANNOUNCES THAT
BISHOP WM. CULBERTSON OF PHILADELPHIA
BECOMES DEAN OF THE EDUCATIONAL DIVISION
SEPTEMBER FIRST." I GO TO JACKSONVILLE VIA
PULLMAN TONIGHT AND LEAVE THERE BY PULL-
MAN FRIDAY NIGHT ARRIVING CHICAGO SUNDAY
MORNING. IF NEEDED TOMORROW PAGE
GEORGE WASHINGTON HOTEL JACKSONVILLE.

WILL H. HOUGHTON

One can well imagine Bishop Culbertson's chagrin at discovering that his resignations in Philadelphia had triggered investigations in Chicago! He was unaccustomed to being an important public figure, and in the years to follow, he would do his best to remain a private man; but he would not always succeed. The Institute press secretary issued a press release on June 11 that was unfortunately not completely accurate. It stated that Bishop Culbertson was "a friend of the late Dr. James M. Gray," when actually Dr. Culbertson's only connection with Dr. Gray was as a listener in congregations where the late Institute president had preached. The release also confused the bishop's educational career by having him take "divinity" training at Temple University (where he actually received his degree in education), and then attending the Reformed Episcopal Seminary following his university studies. He attended the Seminary immediately upon graduation from high school. It was an ecclesiastical technicality, but the release named Howard Higgins as Dr. Culbertson's successor "as rector of the church," when Bishop Higgins was his successor only as bishop.

By the time the announcement had ceased to be news, Dr. Houghton was able to get a letter off to Dr. Culbertson:

> June 15, 1942
>
> We understand very well the mix-up in regard to the announcement. I explained to the Institute family, gathered for chapel this morning, that we would have preferred letting them in on it before the public had word, but that the eastern newspapers were to blame in the matter. All of us can see you are not at fault in any way, so please feel comfortable about it. . . . Let me assure you again of my personal joy in the consummation of this matter, and in the prospect of fellowship in service.

It was no mystery how the news reached the Philadelphia press. The bishop had resigned from the standing committee of the synod on June 9, with the understanding that there would be no public announcement until he had also resigned from the church the next day. But a member of the standing committee jumped the gun and told the press, so that the *Philadelphia Evening Bulletin* carried a story the Wednesday evening Dr. Culbertson resigned from the church! Nobody could miss the caption:

BISHOP WM. CULBERTSON
RESIGNS POSTS HERE
Will Become Dean of Moody
Bible Institute in Chicago

The next day, the *Inquirer* and the *Recorder* also carried stories. Dr. Culbertson was not consulted by the press at any time and was perfectly innocent in the matter. The bishop must have felt helpless as the wheels of publicity turned around him and he could do nothing about it.

Before leaving the matter of his resignations, it would be profitable to consider what he actually said in each case. To the standing committee of the Reformed Episcopal Church he wrote, in part:

Two things need to be said so far as this resignation is concerned. There is a deep and overwhelming conviction in my heart that God is in this move—I confess that I do not see all the possible results, but I have faith to believe that they will be worked out for God's glory and our good. We can only walk by faith, when God makes His will known. The second matter is to point out that I have not the least inclination or desire to sever my relationship with the Reformed Episcopal Church. I am to be free to continue denominational interests. Because I do have in mind the continuance of an active interest, if the Church wants the relationship to be otherwise, it will have to let me know. One feature of my contact with Moody has been the realization that there is absolutely no anti-denominationalism present.

Now to you men who have labored with me, who have stood behind me in such a way as to be a bulwark of strength and power, I want to express my heartfelt thanks. It is not easy to submit my resignation, especially to men who have been so loyal, who have anticipated my desires, who have upheld my hands in every matter; but I must submit my resignation, or else be false to what I believe the will of God is. I want you to know that my heart is with you. And I trust that the blessing of God, which has been upon us in measure in recent years, will continue in greater measure in the years to come. If God has used me in some little measure to continue the efforts toward extension, I am grateful; but my prayer is that greater progress will be the continuing rule of the day. I shall, with God's help, stand with you in prayer. And, though separated by a greater distance than heretofore, I trust that our fellowship shall be renewed from time to time—before you come to Chicago in 1945.

In his letter of resignation addressed to the vestry of the Church of the Atonement, Dr. Culbertson gave this explanation for his decision:

> The future welfare of the Church of the Atonement has been considered by me. There are three things I should like to say about my resignation and the necessity of calling another pastor. First, if God is calling me to Chicago (and I have no doubt that He is), it would be disasterous for me to remain; we could not expect to have God's full blessing, if we were out of His will. Second, I am very much afraid of a long pastorate in which the rector becomes so well loved that, when he is called away, it is an almost impossible task for his successor to do a good work —at least he is hampered, probably for years. Third, I shall be happy to discuss with you the possibilities and qualifications of a successor.

> Because of the overwhelming conviction in my own heart as to the will of God, because I believe that the welfare of the church in the long view will thus best be served, I submit my resignation as rector of the Church of the Atonement, to take effect on August 1, 1942.

One of the vestrymen had some serious misgivings about his pastor's ability to handle the people and the problems at the Institute. He had seen Dr. Culbertson's meekness and gentleness in dealing with church problems, and he wondered if that approach would work in Chicago. He took his pastor aside one evening and shared his concern.

"There are some rugged individualists—even some prima donnas—at the Institute, and they will run roughshod over you. I wonder if you are forceful and positive enough to handle them?"

How did the pastor respond to this advice? The vestryman recalls with a smile, "He graciously thanked me for my advice—which he just as obviously did not need!"

The Culbertson family spent the month of August at their

usual vacation retreat in Mexico, Pennsylvania, about which more will be said later. Before the end of the month, they moved to 530 Forest Avenue, Evanston, Illinois, just north of Chicago. The following year, they moved to 922 Elmwood, and they remained at that address until October, 1964, when Dr. and Mrs. Culbertson moved to Sandburg Village, just one mile north of the Institute on LaSalle Street in Chicago.

There were a few men in the Reformed Episcopal Church who were unhappy with their bishop's decision. They apparently forgot that the possibility of such a move was involved in his decision to become a bishop back in 1937, when he said: "I want it understood that if I'm called to another field of work, and I go, that you won't think I've let you down." If he had remained in Philadelphia, there is no question that his ministry would have been limited. He would have faced the constant tension of local denominational responsibilities and the challenge of the wider conference ministry, a ministry that God was blessing in a signal way. Years later, when his son Paul was ordained in the Reformed Episcopal Church, his father confided in him that there had been some misunderstandings over his decision to go to Chicago. "But where was I to go in the church?" he asked. "I had served three of their churches and taught in the seminary. It seemed like this was the only way to go."

Certainly nobody could have accused him of a selfish ministry. He left a comfortable ministry at Ventnor to go to Germantown where there was no manse and no promise of a salary, and where the church seemed doomed to failure. He left the Church of the Atonement in good shape materially and spiritually, including the addition of a manse. He had been faithful in his work as a bishop and as a teacher, so that his departure from Philadelphia left no shadows behind.

Years before, he had set the sails of his life to be driven by the wind of the Spirit, and now God was leading him into a new and challenging ministry that would touch the lives of millions for years to come.

> *"God being my Helper, in so far as I can influence what goes on at Moody Bible Institute, we are not there to train easy-going Christians; we are there to graduate disciples."*
>
> British Keswick, 1957

FIVE

The Dean

As you drive north along Lake Michigan on Chicago's beautiful Outer Drive, you end up in Evanston, the home of Northwestern University. It was here that the Culbertson family finally located, in a modest, two-story, white frame house on Elmwood Avenue. Joy was twelve years old and Bob nine when they arrived from Philadelphia; Paul had just turned three, and Ruth was twenty-one months old. The children adjusted easily to their new home and eventually came to love the tree-lined avenues and elegant buildings that always seem to characterize a university town.

The location was perfect for Dr. Culbertson. He could drive to the Institute in less than an hour, or take one of the fast commuter trains that serve the northern suburbs of Chicago. Other Institute personnel lived in the same area, so it was possible for them to go back and forth together. Some of the men liked to joke about the dean's "heavy foot," but in reality, he drove carefully and never had a serious accident.

Of course, when the Culbertsons arrived in Chicago, they were welcomed by another exulting letter from Dr. Houghton:

> Welcome to Chicago, to your new home, and to your new work!
>
> If you find any delay in the arrival of your furniture, there are rooms and meals at the Institute for you and your family, so don't go hungry, or sleep out on the lawn!
>
> Please let us know how we can serve you. This part of the world is strange to you, and there may be bits of information you want, errands to be run, etc. Call on us for we are all anxious to help. We want all of you to be comfortable and happy.
>
> This welcome includes your good lady, heartily and unanimously, and the children also, though they probably will not be particularly interested in being welcomed. I hope all of you find the adjustment not too difficult, and that before long every one will love it all.

Dr. Houghton had every reason to rejoice in the arrival of his new dean, for in Dr. Culbertson, he had a man who was as keen spiritually as he was academically. And he was a man deeply concerned about evangelism and missions, two matters that greatly burdened Dr. Houghton's own heart. God had given the Institute an able faculty and staff. Those were the days of Henry Parsons Crowell and his gifted son H. Coleman Crowell; Thomas Smith and his son, Wilbur M. Smith; Dr. P. B. Fitzwater, who was serving as acting dean following the resignation of Dr. Harold Lundquist; Talmage J. Bittikofer; E. C. Christiansen; Homer Hammontree; Harry Dixon Loes; Wendell P. Loveless; Elgin S. Moyer; Max I. Reich, devoted Hebrew-Christian teacher and poet; Kenneth S. Wuest, Greek scholar; and many more. Dr. Houghton's enthusiasm had brought new life to many areas of the ministry, even though because of the war, student recruitment was a bit of a problem. The circulation of *Moody Monthly* had trebled; two new buildings had been constructed; the literature ministry was growing and would lead ultimately to the founding of Moody Press in 1946; and plans were on the president's drawing board for such novel ministries as FM radio and the Moody Institute of Science.

Dr. Houghton introduced the new dean to the ninth floor administrative offices, thoroughly enjoying the experience, as he made humorous remarks to and about the various staff members that he loved so much. He was especially anxious for the new dean to meet Miss May Hogan, who would be his private secretary for the next twenty-nine years. Miss Hogan, a Moody graduate had come back to the Institute in November, 1934, as secretary to Dr. Fitzwater. In 1937, she moved into H. E. Stockburger's office (Institute comptroller); and then in 1940, she became secretary to Dr. Harold Lundquist in the dean's office. When Dr. Lundquist resigned in 1941, Dr. Fitzwater stepped in as acting dean, and Miss Hogan was back to her original job again. She was anxious to meet her new boss, whose message she had so appreciated at the previous Founder's Week conference.

The two men stepped into the dean's office, and Dr. Houghton made the necessary introductions. Then he turned to Dr. Culbertson.

"We need to explain the intercom to you," he said. "Dr. Fitzwater never used it. Every time I would call, he'd say, 'I'll come over and talk!' and hang up. I think he was afraid it would blow up in his face. Anyway, Miss Hogan knows how to work it, and she'll explain it to you."

May Hogan was just a bit skeptical about her new boss, even though she appreciated what she had heard about his ministry. It was his emphasis on "the deeper life" that bothered her. She had heard "deeper life" preaching, and it had not impressed her; and she had met some "deeper life" speakers whose attitudes and actions had prejudiced her greatly against what they taught. But all of that changed when she began working with Dr. Culbertson. Here was a man whose walk with Christ was a practical thing: it touched every area of his life. He was serious but not solemn; even his sense of humor was sanctified, and the two enjoyed many laughs while dealing with the academic problems of a growing school. Sanctity was not a garment he wore on special occasions; it was the hidden fire of his heart that warmed and ignited everything he did.

His years as a bishop had given him opportunity to develop his administrative skills, and it was not long before the Institute family discovered that the new dean knew what he was doing. The problem was that, for some of them, he was not doing it fast enough! "The dean is sitting on it!" became a byword in the administrative offices of Crowell Hall. Accustomed, perhaps, to Dr. Houghton's aggressive administrative methods, Dr. Culbertson's associates were not prepared for the new dean's calm, deliberate approach to getting things done. This does not suggest that the president was wrong and the dean right; it only suggests that different men have different gifts and accomplish the same work by different routes.

The story of Dr. Warren Filkin and his psychology book gives some idea of the adjustments the faculty had to make. Dr. Filkin had come to Moody in January, 1942, and in his elementary psychology class, had inherited a textbook that was published in 1899 and revised slightly in 1920! In those days, "only the Bible" was the textbook in many courses, but elementary psychology was an exception. However, as far as the teacher was concerned, the class would have been better off without a textbook, rather than study one published over forty years before. A Christian friend one day recommended an up-to-date text to Dr. Filkin who, after some weeks of prayerful consideration, wrote a letter to the dean asking his permission to use the newer text.

Dr. Filkin expected to get a reply within a few days, or at the most a week or two; but no reply came. Several months later, he boarded the elevator in Crowell Hall, and there stood Dr. Culbertson. The dean knew that Dr. Filkin was not very excited about teaching the psychology course, so he thought he would joke with him a bit.

"Where have you been, Filkin?" he asked. "Teaching psychology?"

Dr. Filkin knew it was now or never, so he took a chance.

"Dr. Culbertson, I don't insist on teaching psychology. But if I do have to teach it, I would like to have a textbook that is less than forty years old!"

If he had conducted an atomic bomb test in the elevator, the results could not have been more devastating. The other passengers thoroughly enjoyed this administrative banter, and were not hesitant to show it. Before the week was over, Dr. Filkin received the dean's approval for the new book; and, no doubt, the dean enjoyed a good laugh as he wrote the memo. Actually, he and Dr. Filkin were good friends and often shared in the Institute's Bible conference ministry. A few years later, when Dr. Filkin had to go to the hospital for surgery, it was Dr. Culbertson who did the chauffeuring of the patient. But this was not an unusual thing: the dean often showed his concern in a personal way.

The dean was really quite human, in spite of his long-deliberated decisions; and his humanity was best seen on the tennis court or the volleyball court. The tennis courts were located where Houghton Hall now stands, and the gym was in the old 152 building; and Dr. Culbertson regularly made use of both facilities until 1963, when surgery made it necessary for him to limit his strenuous activities. In the early days of his ministry at the Institute, he regularly played volleyball with Warren Filkin, Franklin Broman,

Russell Hitt, Earl Anderson, Harold Cook, and Coach Ockert; and in later years, he took on Wilfred Burton, Don Smith, Bill Pearce, and Coach Nelson. His tennis buddies were Coach Nelson, George Schuler, and David Smart.

The dean was known as a "spiker" in those days, and Harold Cook was his set-up man. On May 19, 1971, when the student body celebrated Culbertson Day, one of the highlights of the program was a presentation by Mr. Cook of a trophy inscribed to Dr. Culbertson as "an outstanding spiker." Dr. Culbertson's response to the tribute was simply, "This is the first trophy I ever got!"

Coach Nelson was not only his partner on the courts; he was also his partner on the greens. One day, the coach wanted to play golf, but the dean had some test papers to grade. Since both of them were teaching Bible geography, they decided to join forces and grade the papers together; so they spread them out on the floor and went to work. About that time, the executive vice-president, Coleman Crowell, and the business manager, H. E. Stockburger, arrived in the dean's office to consult him about a matter; but the dean informed them that he was grading tests and had "an important appointment" when he finished. The men left the office, and as soon as Dr. Culbertson and Coach Nelson finished the papers, they took off for their important appointment—at the golf course.

His fellow sportsmen always kept on their guard in the showers, because it was not unusual for the water suddenly to turn either boiling hot or icy cold. In all fairness, it must be admitted that Dr. Culbertson could take it as well as give it and always enjoyed a good joke.

While possessed of a good sense of humor, Dr. Culbertson was all business when it came to his administrative responsiblities. He conducted faculty meetings with dignity and never allowed his co-workers to forget that they were serving the Lord Jesus Christ and not merely working for an

The boy, Bill, became the man, Dr. William Culbertson, but the smile remained genuine. His firm stand on the Bible was one factor that led him and his family, seen below in 1942, to move to Chicago for his role as dean of the Moody Bible Institute.

William Culbertson's third church was at Germantown, Pennsylvania, the Church of the Atonement. Concurrently, he was bishop of the Reformed Episcopal Church.

Dr. Culbertson enjoyed his family. Above (*from left*), Joy, Dr. Culberston, Mrs. Culbertson, Robert, with Ruth and Paul in front, are at their Evanston, Illinois home. Below, Paul, Robert, and Dr. Culbertson have just returned from a fishing expedition.

The president's chapel every Monday at the Moody Bible Institute was extremely important to Dr. Culbertson, who prepared meticulously for students and staff. As dean in the middle forties, Dr. Culbertson is pictured below with (*front left*) E. C. Christiansen, business manager; H. C. Crowell, executive vice-president; and Dr. Will H. Houghton, president.

Two organizations that received Dr. Culbertson's warm endorsement and participation were (*above*) the Keswick Conference in Great Britain and (*below*) the Accrediting Association of Bible Colleges and Bible Institutes.

Israel had a special fascination for Dr. Culbertson. Here he is examining artifacts at the dig in Jerusalem. In 1969, he, Mrs. Culbertson, and Dr. and Mrs. Ralph Gade also met with David Ben-Gurion, the father of modern Israel.

Whether he traveled to the site of the Korean conflict or visited on a mission field, Dr. Culbertson was always cheerful — and ministered effectively.

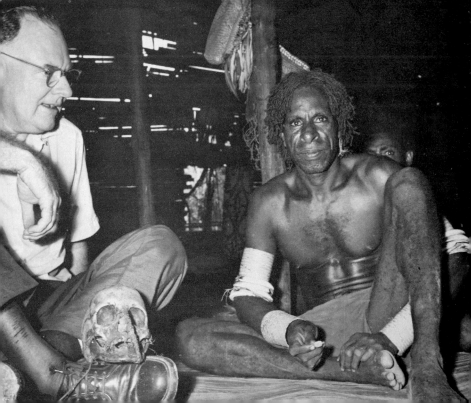

Dr. Culbertson always enjoyed graduation day.

organization. There were discussions, and even disagreements; but the faculty rarely saw the dean become agitated
or upset, nor did they hear him utter a careless or irritable
word. He was not passive; it was just that his deliberate
nature would not permit him the luxury of speaking or acting on the spur of the moment. His oft-repeated counsel,
"Better sleep over it," sometimes irritated them, but in the
long run, they had to admit that his approach was usually
the best one. Of course, the faculty respected their dean,
because they knew he was not only an educator but also a
dedicated scholar, and because he had definite convictions
about the place of the Bible institute in the work of the Lord.
At a faculty retreat, he had this to say:

> What a weighty responsibility is that of the teacher! It is
> serious enough if we miss the way ourselves; it is more seri-
> ous if we lead others astray. Our Lord said: "They are blind
> guides. And if the blind guide the blind, both shall fall into
> a pit" (Mt 15:14, ASV). The teacher, therefore, is not only
> concerned with himself, but—if he has any conscience at
> all—he is concerned that his charges do not fall into a pit.
> This sense of duty is increased when the student is still
> in the pliable age of youth.
>
> There is another side of responsibility: the tremendous
> potentiality of the lives with which we deal. Here, of
> course, is one of the major compensations of the teacher.
> Let us remember, however, that it is within our power to
> make or mar, to help or hinder. We must not only guard
> against misleading students; we must, under God, develop
> the potentiality of each student.

As he saw it, the Christian teacher has a spiritual responsibility in three areas of his ministry: his presentation of the
subject, his speech, and his personal Christian living. Dr.
Culbertson did not see the Christian teacher as a propa-

gandist, but rather as one who presents to his students a true Christian interpretation of life. He continued,

> Our presentation of the Christian view does not exclude and should not exclude a thorough discussion of the non-Christian and anti-Christian positions. College age youth are old enough for this presentation. They need such instruction to face life realistically. They ought to have the benefit of technical advice and specialized supervision in such a study.

His main discussion was under point three, the teacher's spiritual responsibility in his personal Christian living. Here, he emphasized Christian habits of church attendance and interest in spiritual enterprises ("Laxity here will probably lead to failure elsewhere"); Christian courtesy ("especially concerning those who differ on nonessentials"); response to the ministry of the Holy Spirit; personal devotional life; cooperation; diligence in preparation ("ought to be more than the diligence of the unsaved teacher"); ministry for the glory of God; the example of the Christian home; and the fruit of the Spirit. He concluded by saying:

> These are great days! The training of youth is one of the greatest privileges that can be given to a man or woman. Beware of the special pitfalls of your calling: resting on past laurels, indolence, fleshly indulgence, and spiritual apathy. Teaching in a Christian college in days like these should challenge every instructor. Do the best job you can in your field of teaching. Do all that the Lord would have you do in speaking and living. The power of God cannot be displayed through disobedient servants. Pour out your soul in prayer to lead these youths on to the full will of God.

Ever since his courting days, when he and Catharine had debated the relative merits and demerits of the liberal arts college, the Bible institute, and the seminary, he had been formulating his own personal philosophy of Christian education. In one particular message, he said:

Bible institutes from the time of their origin . . . have stressed those things needed for vital Christian witness: the study of the English Bible, the winning of souls, spiritual living, missionary outreach, and gospel hymnody.

While certain elements have been added to the course of study, these basics remain intact. As I see it, the Bible institute is a specialized school, distinct from the liberal arts college, from the theological seminary, and from a scientific institute. Some speak of it as a religious, undergraduate, professional school.

From the beginning, Bible institutes have stressed the practical. Student training has never been limited to the classroom and library. Of course, there is study, plenty of study. Necessarily, there must be instruction both in lecture and dialogue. The riches of books must be entered into in well-stocked and carefully selected libraries. But there is also the experience of actual ministry in churches, clubs, street corners, jails, hospitals, and homes. Taking to others the message of life, sharing the joy of salvation, ministering to those who already believe, and leading souls to the Saviour are part of institute training.

Two other matters need to be emphasized. First, the Bible institute is a school in which the Bible is honored as the inspired Word of God and taught by men utterly committed to the fundamentals of the faith. Second, the Bible institute stresses Christian living. The things which do not make for holy living are to be avoided. The fleshly lusts that war against the soul are to be shunned. Discipline, devotion to duty, sacrificial ministry, the joy and the power of the Holy Spirit—these are part and parcel of Institute life.

> Thank God for all forms of Bible-believing, dedicated Christian education! Each has its place.

He went to the Moody Bible Institute to train men and women to serve Jesus Christ. Their calling was not an easy one; why should their training be easy? Dr. Culbertson was convinced that this preparation was not complete unless it equipped the student to study the Word of God and be able to teach it to others; and this included a knowledge of Bible languages.

> If something can be said for a study of the dead languages in academic education, how much more can be said for such a study in theological education. Many theological schools, particularly those with a liberal emphasis, have relegated the study of the original languages in which the Bible was written to the limbo of forgetfulness. . . . Psychology, sociology, economics, political science came in, and Hebrew and Greek went out. . . . But aside from the kind of subjects which displace the study of Hebrew and Greek, is their displacement really scientific? Our answer is yes, *if* you want a generation of ministers who know nothing of the Bible, who therefore are unable to explain what it means, and who are powerless to defend it. What if some seminary students indolently never use the tool given them! For those who do not use such instruction, there are others who do use it, and there are multitudes who wish they had it.

The school had come a long way since January 22, 1886, when Mr. Moody had said in his Farwell Hall address: "Never mind the Greek and Hebrew, give them plain English and good Scripture." But times had changed too, and the dean was right. After all, he had learned his Greek in high school; and there was no reason why his students could not learn it *after* high school!

As is often the case, a servant of God makes a decision and acts upon it, and then other opportunities present themselves. On December 2, 1943, the chairman of the board of the Philadelphia School of the Bible wrote Dr. Culbertson that the directors had voted unanimously to invite him to become president of the school. It was no secret to the board members that the late president, J. Davis Adams, had expressed his desire that William Culbertson succeed him; and there were some definite factors that could easily draw the dean back to his native Philadelphia. He was familiar with the school, having taught there for fourteen years; and he was appreciated by the evangelical Christians in the area. Had he followed his own human inclinations, he would have accepted the invitation; but he and his wife laid the matter before the Lord and waited for His direction. It was not long in coming: ten days later, he wrote to the chairman:

> Both Mrs. Culbertson and I have been very certain of the Lord's leading in bringing us to Chicago. This conviction is all the deeper, since the Lord has so remarkably met us in this our first experience in so great a removal from all whom we knew in close fellowship—both of kith and kin. Moreover, the opportunity at the Moody Bible Institute is a very large one—and one which I have hardly begun to enter. Consequently, though there is a strong human tug to return to Philadelphia, we cannot escape the conviction that the Lord's place is here. It is not that the opportunity in Philadelphia is unattractive, but rather that we dare not remove ourselves from the place where we have been so clearly led and happily blessed of the Lord.

SIX

The Death of Dr. Houghton

The combined ministries of teaching in the classroom, guiding the academic affairs of the Institute, and ministering the Word in conferences and churches greatly delighted Dr. Culbertson; and he would have rejoiced to see the Lord keep him in this kind of ministry, but it was not to be. Will Houghton was a sick man, far more seriously than most people realized. For years, he had been plagued with migraine headaches, and they were growing more severe and more frequent. His dedication to Christ and his determination kept him going, even when tortured by pain; but it could not continue. Little by little, Dr. Culbertson assisted his beloved friend by assuming some of his responsibilities and helping to carry the administrative burdens as much as he could.

On June 4, 1946, Dr. Houghton had a serious coronary and was rushed to the Presbyterian Hospital in Chicago. He remained there until July 18, when he returned home; but he was not seen in his office very frequently. He and his wife spent six weeks in the Pacific Northwest, returning to Chicago on October 1; but again, he was not strong enough to take up the work that he loved and sorely missed. He and the dean were in close and constant communication, so the organizational wheels were still turning. The entire Institute was praying much and working hard, and God was blessing. Dr. Houghton gave his last chapel message on November 4. His opening statement was, "Remember me? I'm Will Houghton!"

The next months were spent in a determined effort to restore his ebbing health. Late in November, he was taken to Hot Springs, Arkansas; but there was no change. Just before Christmas, he and Mrs. Houghton went to Tucson, and he seemed to rest better. On April 7, 1947, they travelled to California; and on June 13, Dr. Houghton's condition was so improved that they decided to return to Chicago. Later that day, however, a severe headache developed, and the hotel physician was summoned. In spite of an injection to lessen the pain, the condition persisted and then grew worse; and the coronary followed. Dr. Houghton was taken to the Hollywood Receiving Hospital, where he died early Saturday morning, June 14.

The Institute family was stunned when they received the news, since most of them had heard that their president was much improved and was on his way back to Chicago. The official announcement was made over WMBI and WDLM at two o'clock Saturday afternoon; and before long, messages of sympathy began to arrive not only from the listening area, but from many parts of the country. The news was spreading fast, and the impact of it was touching not only the Institute family in general, but the dean in particular. "I feel as though I've lost a father," he commented. His words for a special edition of the *Moody Student*, published the following Monday, were:

> It is a great loss, for Dr. Houghton was a great leader under God, a man who naturally commanded respect. We all had great respect for his judgment, because he lived close to the Lord, and that's the kind of thing that money can't buy—that you just don't find anywhere. That is the burden on my heart.

If he was sincerely trying to express himself without completely revealing what was in his heart, the dean failed; because it is clear that he was asking himself—and had been asking for weeks—"Where will we find another leader like

Dr. Houghton?" It probably never entered his mind that *he* would be Dr. Houghton's successor. If it did, he no doubt smiled, shook his head, and started thinking about something else!

The Institute trustees met in emergency session on Thursday and appointed Dr. William Culbertson acting president of the school. The next day, thousands of people arrived at the Institute to pay their final respects to Dr. Houghton whose body lay in state in the reception room of the 830 building. Early that afternoon, the body was moved to the Moody Memorial Church, one mile north on LaSalle Street, where the funeral service was scheduled for two-thirty. More than three thousand people attended the service, which was led by Dr. Culbertson, assisted by Moody Church pastor, Dr. H. A. Ironside, and Dr. Weldon M. Wilson, pastor of the North Shore Baptist Church, where Dr. and Mrs. Houghton were members. Dr. Wilson read Scripture from 1 Corinthians 15 and John 14, and Dr. Ironside made some personal remarks and led in prayer. James P. Davies led the Moody Chorale in the singing of "God Leads His Dear Children Along" and "Songs in the Night," one of Dr. Houghton's own compositions.

From the very beginning of his address, Dr. Culbertson sounded a note of faith and courage.

> The message that our Lord had called unto Himself His servant, Dr. Houghton, not only left us saddened, it left us stunned. It seemed difficult to pierce the darkness of bewilderment. It was hard to see God's providential care; for the moment it seemed that we were desolate. Then our Heavenly Father began to speak in and through the grief which He permitted to come. We do not need to *see*, it is enough to know; it is better to know, for that knowledge rests in who God is; sight is limited, knowledge transcends sight. Even when we do not see, "We know

that all things work together for good to them that love God, to them who are the called according to his purpose."

Instead of delivering a eulogy ("one thing above another that Dr. Houghton would not want"), the dean read passage after passage from the late president's own writings, particularly his songs and poems. He closed by saying,

There is confidence in the darkest hour, for God is on the throne. We, therefore, take heart. The God of Moody, of Torrey, of Gray, of Crowell, and of Houghton, still lives!

Dr. Culbertson, along with other Institute officers, accompanied the body to New Bethlehem, Pennsylvania, where, at three-thirty Saturday afternoon, the final rites were held at the First Baptist Church, where Dr. Houghton had pastored in 1918. The funeral message by the dean again was positive and optimistic, based on three "We know" statements from the New Testament, 2 Timothy 1:12, Romans 8:28, and 2 Corinthians 5:1. Dr. Culbertson was not certain *how* God would provide the school with a president, but that He *would* meet the need, he had absolutely no doubt. He had waited upon the Lord at crisis hours before, and he would wait upon Him now even more.

"It has been a sad privilege in some respects to have the place of leadership God has given me."

Founder's Week, 1958

SEVEN

The President

Back in Chicago, William Culbertson sadly returned to his own office and took up the dual responsibilities of dean and acting president.

"Why don't you move into the president's office?" Coleman Crowell asked him, "After all, you're doing the work."

But William Culbertson had no designs either upon the title or the newly vacated office facilities. As far as he was concerned, God had called him to serve temporarily as acting president, and in His good time He would bring in a new leader. He enjoyed his work as dean and teacher and expected to continue serving in this way. He and Catharine often talked about the matter, and prayed about it, and it was no secret that both of them wanted the dean to stay right where he was.

One morning, the dean arrived at his office and discovered an unlighted firecracker on his chair.

"Who put this here?" he asked Miss Hogan.

"I think it was Mr. Coleman Crowell," she replied. "He wants to get you over to the president's office!"

"Where did he go?" the dean inquired.

"I think he went to the men's room down the hall."

74

The dean hurried out the door and in a minute rushed to his desk and quickly sat down. In a few seconds, there was a muffled explosion, followed by Coleman Crowell bolting out of the men's room with a bewildered look on his face. He was sure the dean had tossed the lighted firecracker into the men's room, but the benign look on Dr. Culbertson's face disarmed him.

In a July 16, 1947 letter to the friends of the Institute, Dr. Culbertson wrote:

> Dr. Houghton's homegoing leaves a vacancy which can never really be filled. But the God of Moody, Torrey, Gray and Houghton still lives, and for each one of us this is an hour of reconsecration to Him and His work here. . . . My appointment as acting president of the Institute has given me a fresh sense of my inadequacy apart from His strength.
>
> Moody Bible Institute will carry on, true to the Word of God, loyal to the Son of God.

Had Dr. Culbertson given the least hint that he was interested in being president, the trustees would no doubt have elected him much sooner; but no hints were given. Why? Simply because he did not feel at that time that he was the man God had chosen for the office. Except in their devotion to Christ, you could not find two more opposite men than William Culbertson and Will H. Houghton. "I know that Dr. Culbertson hesitated to take on the responsibility, because he felt he was more of an academic person than he was an administrator," explains MBI trustee W. Maxey Jarman. "Dr. Houghton had been much more of a flamboyant type with great imagination." It was general knowledge among Institute personnel that Dr. Houghton could think up more new ideas in an hour than the staff could implement in a month. Dr. Culbertson's approach was different, and he sensed this difference. And perhaps, he and Catharine had a fleeting hope that one day God would call them back into the pastorate; and it would be difficult to leave the president's office for a move like that.

For nearly a year, the trustees prayed and waited and, on occasion, considered various men for the president's office. Fifteen different men were carefully considered and rejected. And the enemy was at work during those difficult months, seeking to undermine the school and discredit it before its many friends around the world.

For one thing, four faculty members resigned, not because of any special problems at the school, but simply because God had opened other doors of ministry for them. It was unfortunate that their resignations coincided with Dr. Houghton's homegoing, because this gave the impression that there was no leadership left at the school. Rumors began to fly that the entire faculty was leaving and that the ministry was going to be cut back, especially in the area of publishing. There is something about the public—including the Christian public—that makes it easy to accept a rumor and difficult to desire the truth; and the sad result was a decrease in giving. Paradoxically, at the same time the funds were getting low, a rumor made the rounds that the Institute was really very rich in endowments, and a number of people actually wrote to the stewardship department asking for financial help for their "ministries."

Perhaps some of these incidents were in the back of Dr. Culbertson's mind when he gave his 1957 Founder's Week message:

> Incidentally, have you ever noticed—I say it to our shame —how quick we are to believe the worst about someone? God help us! Some idle word of gossip and our ears are alert and our minds are feverishly active. God help us!

But the school weathered the storm, and the trustees continued to seek for the president of God's choosing. Early in 1948, there was a growing conviction among them that God's chosen man was Dr. William Culbertson; and on Wednesday, February 4, the entire board met and elected him president.

"I'm terribly sorry, but I can't make it for dinner tonight," he explained to Catharine over the phone. "The trustee meeting lasted longer than I expected, and then there's the service this evening. I'll get home as soon as I can." There was a brief pause, and then he added in a casual way, "The trustees elected me president of the Institute today."

Thomas S. Smith, vice-chairman of the board, made the announcement to all the employees at a special meeting that afternoon; and it was received with applause and the spontaneous singing of the Doxology.

"After much prayer for guidance during the past months," Smith said, "I am happy to say that as a unit, we elected Dr. Culbertson. We thank God for him. We love him. We know God's power is upon him. We believe the greatest days are yet ahead."

In his usual self-effacing manner, Dr. Culbertson replied: "I cannot take Dr. Houghton's place. But I want to be in God's will. I want to be in the place God wants me to be. Moody Bible Institute can be a power for God as each one of us is in the place God can use us. One encouragement is the fact that I have the love and devotion and prayers of you people. You are close to my heart. I think you know that, and I sense you have taken me into your hearts. How I thank God for that.

"It is wonderful for Mr. Smith to say that the best years are yet ahead. I believe it is possible, if we are in the place God wants us to be. We have a great God. Let us go ahead with Him! We have had many evidences of His working in these past months, and I know we will experience the power of God as we go on with Him.

"I know I may count on you. Let us pray one for the other."

The trustees picked a good time for the announcement: it was the day before D. L. Moody's birthday. Had William Culbertson been an impulsive man, the announcement would have been made nine months before. But he wanted to be sure. "I cannot take Dr. Houghton's place. But I want to be in God's will." It was another one of those costly decisions, and he had made them before. It was that kind of a decision that took him from the joys of Ventnor, New Jersey, to the difficulties of Germantown, Pennsylvania, and that made him agree to be a candidate for bishop when it appeared that a man was needed at a critical hour. A similar decision had taken him from Philadelphia to Chicago, though it meant being misunderstood by some and criticized by others. There was a work to be done, and God had chosen him to do it. He simply wanted to give God the time to make His will clear to His servant. Now God's will was clear, and he obeyed by faith.

The inauguration was held at the Moody Memorial Church on May 13, with Frank F. Taylor, chairman of the board of trustees, presiding. The service opened with the singing of "All Hail The Power of Jesus' Name," followed by S. Maxwell Coder, acting dean of education, reading Scripture from Deuteronomy 28:1-14, and P. B. Fitzwater leading in prayer. The trustees selected the Moody Church pastor, Dr. H. A. Ironside, to give the charge to Dr. Culbertson. It was an impressive service, as Dr. Ironside first charged the new president to be true to the faith and to the purposes of the school, and then charged the Institute employees, alumni, and students to be equally faithful in their support of the president. The address was given by Dr. Culbertson's former pastor, Harold S. Laird, who at that time was pastor of the Independent Presbyterian Church, Wilmington, Delaware. President of the Alumni Association, Lawrence E. Pearson, gave the benediction.

The May 24 issue of *Newsweek* carried a sympathetic story about the Institute and its new president. It said in part:

> Bishop Culbertson (he retains his denominational post) is a large, plain, and cheerful man. He thinks of himself less as an evangelist in the Dwight Moody tradition than as an administrator and educator. Where Moody the layman was a splendid businessman, Culbertson the minister will leave most financial matters to his subordinates. His comment on his appointment by the board of trustees was: "I want to be in the place God wants me to be."

During twenty-three years of ministry as president, Dr. Culbertson would feel the energetic shadow of Will H. Houghton over him. Houghton *was* "an evangelist in the Dwight Moody tradition," and it was this contrast in personalities and ministries that had made it so difficult for Dr. Culbertson to decide. It seems that everybody but the president felt he was qualified for the office! An editorial in the *Moody Church News,* shortly after his election to office, said:

> The Board of Directors of the Moody Bible Institute are to be congratulated on the sound judgment they have manifested in electing Dr. William Culbertson to be President of that great Bible training school. Ever since the lamented death of Dr. Will H. Houghton, Dr. Culbertson has been Acting President, but we now rejoice that he has been definitely called to and has accepted the office of President. We know of no one better fitted for that position. His deep spirituality, his intimate acquaintance with the Word of God, his scholarly background and recognized administrative ability qualify him to head up that work in a worthy way. We have always considered it a striking evidence of Dr. Houghton's judgment of men when he ventured to ask Dr. Culbertson to relinquish his position as a bishop in the Reformed Episcopal Church, in order to become dean of the Moody Bible Institute. It was a rare evidence of

humility and recognition of the call of God that led the
bishop to take this step—a step which many would consider as a downward one, but which evidently in the mind
of God was a move upward. His years of association with
Dr. Houghton enabled him to enter fully into the hopes
and aspirations of that great man of God, and we feel
sure he will carry on in a worthy way the work that Dr.
Houghton planned.

That same year, Dr. Ironside resigned from the Moody
Church pastorate to devote himself to a full-time conference
ministry; and two years later, the Moody Church asked
Dr. Culbertson if he would consider becoming their pastor.
In refusing the call, Dr. Culbertson wrote:

> In all my prayer and contemplation there has loomed
> largely before me the fact that the Lord led me to the
> Moody Bible Institute. Of that leading there have been
> many clear evidences. As yet there are no indications of
> God's will, which I can discover, that I should move. In
> ascertaining God's will, I have looked for some sense of a
> finished work or other indication that I should change, as
> well as taking into consideration a new opportunity. As
> best I can, I try not to let the largeness or the smallness of
> an opportunity, as I judge it, be the deciding factor in the
> decision. Particularly do I look for that settled peace, that
> conviction of heart that makes me content that it is right to
> leave as well as right to go.
>
> Because I do not sense a finished task at the Institute I
> must regretfully reply in the negative to your request.
> Thank you for your thought of me. For the man of God's
> choice I know it will be a joy and a privilege to work side
> by side with you in the great work the Lord has given
> Moody Church.

History was repeating itself. First, the challenge of a difficult work; then the weeks of prayer and consideration;

then the decision. And once the decision was made, another call! When he became dean of the Institute, he was invited to become president of the Philadelphia School of the Bible. Now he was president of the Institute, and the pulpit of one of the world's most famous churches was opened to him. Actually, his quiet ministry of Bible teaching would have made him a perfect successor to Dr. Ironside; but it was the will of God that he succeed Will H. Houghton. But before too many years, Dr. Culbertson would make his own mark upon the Institute, just as his predecessors had done; and God would use him to build a ministry.

There were many facets to his ministry as president, and the best way to appreciate them is to consider them individually.

"We pledge ourselves to offer the same God-owned curriculum which God has blessed and which has been used of God in the preparation of thousands of Christian workers at home and abroad."

MBI assembly
October 6, 1965

EIGHT

The Administrator

"William Culbertson moved the Moody Bible Institute out of the nineteenth century and into the twentieth century."

So said Dr. S. Maxwell Coder, who became dean of education after Dr. Culbertson moved into the office of president. It was not an extravagant statement. The original curriculum was established in 1889, and no major changes were made until 1895 when the "three course plan" was instituted. Students could select the Bible course, the music course, or the practical Christian work course. Five years later, the missionary course was added; and in 1906, there was a minor overhaul of the program, primarily a rearranging of subjects and some changes in terminology. In 1925, the program underwent its third reorganization in an attempt to simplify what was gradually becoming a rather complex thing; but the changes were primarily organizational and not in terms of content or philosophy.

There were a number of one-hour courses in the curriculum, and both the president and the dean felt it was necessary to combine them into three- and four-hour courses. For one thing, students were having a difficult time transferring credit to other schools, and, on the practical side, it was frightening for a student to face a possibility of thirteen finals at the end of the year!

The second major change had to do with the establishing of a standard three-year program for all students. The Pastor's course had been a three-year course for many years, but most of the other courses were only two years in length. This made it possible to add many more Bible subjects to the curriculum, an improvement that greatly pleased Dr. Culbertson.

But the third change was even more drastic. The Institute had been on the term plan, with three terms of fourteen weeks each. Because of this, it was out of step with most other schools; and during the third quarter, very few students were able to enter. Since the end of the war, when most other schools were booming, the Institute was actually declining in enrollment; and both the president and the dean felt that the term plan was partly to blame. If a student wanted to transfer from another school, the Moody calendar made this very difficult. When the school changed to the semester plan and instituted a summer school program, enrollment began to increase, so much so that the school had to lease the entire sixth floor of the nearby Lawson YMCA to house the large number of men who were attending. It took only two years for the school to make the transitions necessary: the old students stayed with their original program until they graduated, and the new students entered in the new program.

In the early 1960s, a great deal of pressure was put upon Dr. Culbertson to make the Institute a Bible college and begin granting degrees. This kind of pressure was not new; as far back as 1931, the pastoral students were petitioning Dr. Gray to have the school award the bachelor's degree to graduates of the pastor's course. In a letter dated July 27, 1931, and signed by sixty students, the men presented their case for a degree:

1. It would attract college students to the Institute and perhaps prevent them from studying at liberal seminaries.

2. It would encourage graduates to go on for further education after graduation.

3. It would give graduates more recognition in their various denominations. "Today there are men in the graduating class who will have to leave their denomination, unless they go to a seminary and obtain the degree, which would mean they would be duplicating the work they received here."

4. It would bring "more recognition and respect to the Institute from denominations."

5. "A degree is only a fair reward to men who have labored three long years of eleven months each, whereas in any seminary of three years of only seven months each they receive this recognition."

6. How can graduates recommend the Institute to friends who plan to go to seminary anyway?

7. Some seminaries are not "turning out soul-winners" and this is why the school was founded. "We believe that if Mr. Moody were living today he would recognize the need and would include here a course giving a degree which would be recognized by denominations."

The men listed four more reasons which were actually but a rephrasing of reasons already given, and then closed with this appeal:

> We desire the degree, not as an end in itself, but as a means to an end, that we might stand anywhere and everywhere, and preach or teach God's living Word, full of the Holy Spirit, and at the same time make men know we can "give a reason for the hope that is within us": not only from a scriptural standpoint, but also as to their own high

standards of education and be used of God to win the well-educated as well as the less-educated men to Christ.

Dr. Gray shared the letter with the faculty and invited them to express their views in writing. He discussed these evaluations with the trustees at their November meeting. Dr. Harold Lundquist took each argument individually and knocked it down. But after all, Dr. Lundquist had been able, during his years of training, to transfer Institute credit to Princeton Seminary, and if Princeton did it, other schools could do it too! And the idea that a man with a degree can better evangelize the educated was "contradicted by the entire life and ministry of D. L. Moody."

Dr. P. B. Fitzwater handed in an eight-page analysis worthy of his keen mind. "The grave question must be met as to whether to meet such conditions [necessary for the granting of degrees] would not frustrate the purpose of God in the founding of the Institute." Oscar Lowry, in his report, apologized to the trustees that he could not come before them "as a college graduate," but only as a humble graduate of the Institute itself. He then cited eight reasons why he was against the proposition of granting degrees, beginning with, "I do not believe that any such thing was ever intended by God, or the man who [*sic*] God used to found this institution," and ending with, "Whenever the Moody Bible Institute ceases to major in evangelism and turns to scholasticism her doom is sealed so far as fulfilling the original purpose and mission for which this institution was organized."

A. F. Gaylord, who had been closely associated with D. L. Moody, had some real ammunition.

How well I remember Mr. Moody saying, when he was appealed to on more than one occasion to introduce secular education in the Institute for students who might be more efficient workers, "Let those who specialize along those lines do that—we will stick to the Bible and emphasize that, for the need is so urgent. We can get men and women to teach everything else but we cannot get men and women to teach the Bible. Let us train them for that purpose."

He also remembered what Moody had said to Torrey on one occasion:

"Torrey, I shall turn over in my grave if that time ever comes when the practical work is cut out or we cease to emphasize the Word of God and try to take the place of the seminaries. They have their place—our business is to teach the Bible and know how to win men to Jesus Christ."

Dr. Torrey had shared this same burden with Mr. Gaylord:

Doctor Torrey again and again talked with me deploring the fact that so many things were being introduced into the curriculum of the Institute, saying that first and last it should be a Bible Institute where the Bible was expounded and students received a training and an ability to teach it and set on fire for God and winning of souls.

Then Gaylord concluded,

Granting degrees at the present time will only be the thin edge of the wedge and in days to come, when the present management is gone, emphasis without doubt will be far afield from what has given the Moody Bible Institute the testimony that she now enjoys.

I greatly regret the appeal for granting of degrees and earnestly hope that the same zeal and effort that is being put forth along those lines might be put forth in imparting a more thorough knowledge of the Word of God, a vision for lost souls and the exaltation of Jesus Christ and shall continue in prayer that the Trustees shall be led aright in their decision.

Archibald R. Wright was upset at the students' conviction that, if Mr. Moody were alive, he would agree with their request. For them to make such a statement, said Mr. Wright, was "to be guilty of a purely gratuitous, unfounded and arrogant assumption of the most egotistical character." Of course, the petitioning students were handicapped and "are to be forgiven because they are young men of immature thought and with little background of knowledge concerning Mr. Moody and the work which God gave him to do." He then added a new argument that perfectly suited him as the manager of the business affairs of the school: any changes would definitely affect the donors. The people gave because they felt the school was fulfilling the purposes established by D. L. Moody.

> When you change the character of the Moody Bible Institute, you must create a new type of donor, who will take the place of the Godly, Bible loving men and women of separated lives unto God, who will largely cease their gifts if the petition submitted today is granted.

Dr. Gray wrote to the president of the class that had submitted the petition:

> The Trustees have given the petition most careful consideration, but while appreciating its arguments and admiring the ability and courtesy in which they were presented, they nevertheless request me to inform you that your request is not granted. . . . The granting of degrees appears to them contrary to the genius of the Moody Bible Institute, and they fear its tendency might be to magnify the natural and lessen the supernatural in our work, thus diverting it from the higher and broader objective of its founder under God, Dwight L. Moody.

> We would spare you if we could, the disappointment this decision may bring to your young hearts, for our interest in you is deep and abiding. It is our hope, however, that

you will not only respect the decision, but that in the retro-
spect you will accord it your commendation.

Thirty years later, the president, dean, and trustees were
facing the same issue; but this time, the impetus came from
the administration and not the student body. In 1960, Dr.
Culbertson had inaugurated a self-study program with a
view to improving the academic standards of the school,
and the question of granting degrees was repeatedly
brought up. In 1962, he and Dr. Coder sent a questionnaire
to all students who had attended since 1954 to see how they
felt about the total program. Dr. Coder had quietly been
gathering relevant information, including all the pros and
cons that he heard in faculty meetings, cabinet meetings,
and the informal conversations that are always found on a
campus. In his annual report to the trustees, dated January
15, 1963, he included four pages of information on the subject of degrees. He was careful at the very outset to assure
the officers that he had no desire to change the character of
the school. He wrote:

> The uniqueness of Moody Bible Institute must be pre-
> served. It is today subject to pressures that it change its
> course, that it become like thousands of other schools
> which surround it in our nation, that it seek to win the
> favor of secular educators by diluting its peculiar emphases
> through the introduction of purely cultural subjects in the
> field of general education. We have entered another
> time of crisis for the Institute, when decisions must be
> made which demand clear insight into the complex prob-
> lems surrounding our future.

He then wisely reviewed some of the changes that had been
made in the past, changes that apparently had not hindered
the effectiveness of the school.

Some twenty years ago a changing educational pattern in

the United States forced us to break with tradition and to require high school graduation for entrance to our Day School. It soon became clear that God gave wisdom to the Faculty and Administration at the time that important action was taken.

A dozen years ago, further changes in the educational climate of America had produced a declining enrollment at the Institute. We introduced the most significant changes ever made in our history, by adopting the semester plan, revising our curriculum and standardizing on a three year program of study. This was immediately followed by a dramatic upsurge in enrollments, as God set His seal upon the changes we had made. . . . During the years when we have been consolidating these gains, further changes have been taking place outside the Institute which seem to call for additional changes in our own program. Perhaps the most important factor with which we must contend today is the demand, by evangelical young people and by Christian organizations, for degrees as the hallmark of academic preparation.

He then outlined briefly the possible choices the school would have to face in the future: maintain the status quo, which could weaken the school's ministry; go to a four-year college course, which the dean did not recommend himself; or go to the "3-2 plan" and grant a degree when the graduate completes two years at a recognized college or university. It was a masterful presentation of a difficult and emotionally charged topic, and there is little doubt that Dr. Coder and Dr. Culbertson had often discussed the matter.

Two weeks later, Dr. Culbertson received a bulky file from trustee Robert E. Nicholas, with a covering letter that said:

In view of the question concerning degrees, perhaps the enclosed material of the pros and cons of the battle of

1931 may be of interest to you. I confess I haven't read it since "those days."

Whether D. L. Moody was turning over in his grave, as he told Dr. Torrey he would do, nobody could be sure; but a multitude of ideas were being turned over in the Institute executive offices, and the outcome was the establishment of the degree program in 1965.

Of course, Dr. Culbertson was not impulsive as he weighed the factors and worked with his staff in gathering information. The faculty met each Monday afternoon at two-thirty, and from time to time, the degree program was discussed, with Dr. Coder taking careful notes for his own benefit. The issue was also taken up in the weekly cabinet meetings. (Dr. Coder called the cabinet meetings "the bloody pit," not because the men lacerated each other, but because they honestly bared their hearts without reservation as they considered matters that related to the work of the school. "It was a remarkable device to keep MBI on an even keel," Dr. Coder observed.) Meeting weekly in the cabinet with the president were the executive vice-president, Henry C. Crowell, and the vice-presidents, S. Maxwell Coder, Harold E. Stockburger, and Robert L. Constable. More than once, the men heard the president say, "Well, we'll sleep on it. The Lord will show us which way to go."

After the presentation of Dr. Coder's brief summary of January 1963, nothing more was put into print until October 1964, when Dr. Coder gave the president a twenty-five page analysis of the problem. Unlike his 1963 summary, which was tentative and exploratory, this one opened with the bold recommendation that "the Moody Bible Institute should offer degrees for the successful completion of a three-year program of study plus two years of acceptable work at a recognized liberal arts college or university." He listed twenty-eight reasons why the program should be adopted, the first one being (all the arguments of 1931 not-withstanding): "Our historic single objective would be preserved."

Dr. Culbertson studied the report carefully, as the penciled notations in the margin indicate. He did not agree with everything in the report, but he had to admit that the dean had done his homework well. The two men often discussed the problem, and together they prayed for God's direction. Everyone knew that Dr. Culbertson loved "the old paths," that he was reticent to make changes, unless they were for the good of the ministry in the will of God. A note from missions instructor Harold R. Cook indicated that faculty leaders were strongly in favor of the change. It is interesting to compare Mr. Cook's observations with those given to Dr. Gray thirty years before.

I like the proposed plan for various reasons:
1. It maintains the distinctiveness of our contribution.
2. It recognizes the need to adapt to today's needs.
3. It does not offer more than we are able to provide.
4. It is not a radical departure but the next step in the course we were already pursuing.
5. It is not the sort of program that will attract the wrong kind of students to any significant degree,
6. Neither will it attract the wrong kind of teachers.
7. It leaves the door open for further developments in line with our objectives.

The president "slept on it" some more, and then on May 3, 1965, he read a paper to the faculty that summarized his thinking to date. First, he explained the problems of their present program: young people are increasingly desiring degrees and so are the agencies that employ them. The Institute lost some outstanding applicants who enrolled in schools granting degrees, and student drop-outs were on the increase. Was a four-year program the answer? No it was not.

It would require a basic change in the objectives of the school and, in the long run, would "secularize the campus." The Institute would then be competing with denominational colleges and seminaries, something that Mr. Moody and his successors always tried to avoid.

He listed eighteen advantages of the five-year program, most of which came from Dr. Coder's report of October 1964. Then he expanded on the theme, facing each problem honestly and coming up with answers that were more than satisfactory. The last point in his paper was "The Need for Decisive Action." The president might "sleep on it" for a while, but when he knew the right course, he immediately moved into action!

> The plan here suggested is believed to be distinctive and creative. It may well set the pattern for the best in Bible education in the future. We must see to it that every recipient of a degree shall have not only our established academic program of training in Bible and related fields, but also a cultural background which goes beyond that which would be possible in any shorter program of combined Bible and liberal arts studies. Our degree graduates must be able to take their places with graduates of leading universities as having the broad general education expected of leaders in today's world.

> The annual report of the school to the Trustees for 1962 concluded by quoting a paragraph from *Forbes* which had appeared in a recent article. A discussion of Coca Cola's break with a traditional but obsolete formula for a profitable business closed with the comment:
>> *Moral*: Fortunate is the corporation whose bosses have the courage and objectivity to sense the need for change before it is forced upon them by disaster.
> Fortunate indeed will our school be if we have the courage and good judgment to make whatever changes are needed to preserve the integrity and leadership of our school in the difficult days ahead.

The bishop was sure that Mr. Moody was not turning over in his grave.

At the trustees meeting, September 28, 1965, Dr. Culbertson presented the recommendation from the executive committee that the school grant degrees. It was a brief paper, only three pages long; but on a fourth page, stapled to the others, the president wrote for his own use:

1. Note increase in Bible content.
2. No relaxation on requirements
     plus
3. Two years of secular training.

To recognize not only the need for remaining faithful to purpose, *yet* to recognize need for further training which is expected by so many churches and mission boards AND also expected by academic institutions beyond liberal arts such as seminaries.

The recommendation was accepted. Dr. Culbertson then sat down with a blank sheet of notebook paper and wrote out the official announcement that was finally made at a school assembly, October 6, 1965, opening with a sentence that was typically Dr. Culbertson: "After long and prayerful study, the Institute trustees, administration and faculty have decided to grant bachelor degrees."

There were those who felt the decision was wrong, and some of the ghosts of 1931 came back to haunt him. But the school did not become "secularized," nor did the friends of the school cease to support it. There seemed to be no magnifying of the natural and lessening of the supernatural. Perhaps had the decision been made thirty years before, these things would have happened; but they did not happen in 1965. Dr. Gray had the courage to maintain the status quo in the will of God, and Dr. Culbertson had the courage to change it in the will of God. Had he been in the president's chair in 1931, no doubt Dr. Culbertson would have made the same decision Dr. Gray made, and with the same motive: to preserve the ministry of the school.

*"We need a knowledge—a deeper
knowledge—of the Word of God; and
I take it that most of you understand
that and are longing for a more profound understanding of the Word of
God, or you wouldn't be at a school
like Moody Bible Institute."*

Chapel address
October 12, 1970

NINE

The Shepherd

Above everything else, William Culbertson considered himself a preacher of God's Word; and more important than any other preaching engagement was his chapel time with the Moody students each Monday morning. If you had examined the contents of his desk drawers during those years, you would have found outlines of chapel messages on filing cards, the backs of envelopes, odd-sized pieces of scrap paper, and even corners ripped from larger sheets. One specimen measures 1¾" by 3", and has on it in the president's distinctive script the numbers of the hymns to be used, references to four Bible passages, and ten words related to the outline. Across the tiny page is written "chapel 7/22/51." It is difficult to believe that from such a meager outline, anybody could lead a chapel program and deliver a message; but William Culbertson did it week after week, with no diminishing of his spiritual power.

The students came to chapel expecting meat and not milk, and they were not disappointed. To be sure, some of them were not always able to digest the rich meal immediately; but in years to come, they discovered that their spiritual stature had grown just the same. Often he received letters from graduates telling him how helpful the chapel messages had been to them, and it was not unusual for him to receive a note from a student still on campus.

> I am writing this note in appreciation for your Monday morning chapel services. Many times they have been an inspiration for me to start another week.

> In particular, may I thank you for the past two on joy and peace. Last Sunday night I returned to school from Women's Glee Club tour, which was very hard for me. A letter from home with bad news awaited me. . . . I hardly felt like beginning classes the next morning. Things from all directions began to fall beneath me with disappointments. The chapel that morning in Galatians 5, and the fruits of joy and peace, meant so much to me. Not only me, but many of us needed that message of encouragement.

Stephen Olford put it accurately when he said, "You sensed reality in his preaching." His manner was serious and deliberate, at times even solemn; and you knew that his message came from the overflow of his heart. He had compassion, and his congregations knew it. Something he said in his 1954 Founder's Week message helps us better understand how he prepared his messages.

> As I waited before God, this message was not prepared without tears, God knows! As He searched this old heart of mine, as He spoke deeply to my soul, as I faced what the Word of God has to say about the necessity of reality as an evidence that we know Him, I couldn't escape the fact that God wanted me to say this to you.

In his 1958 message, he had this warning for his fellow ministers:

> Mark it, Christian leader; mark it, pastor. Until it touches you, it won't touch anybody to whom you minister. I haven't learned very much, but one thing I have learned, that if I minister to people, God ministers to them about the same thing He has to talk to me about. And until He has talked to me about it, it is just clanging cymbals and empty words.

He emphasized it in a different way in a 1957 address at British Keswick.

> I can only say that out of my own experience, it is not until I have been quiet, and I have been still, and waited in the presence of God, that I have sensed the reality of God.

His Bible study was worship, and his preaching was not only before men, but, above all else, before God. For this reason, he often refused Sunday evening preaching opportunities so that he might have adequate time on the Lord's Day to prepare himself to minister to his "sons and daughters" in chapel on Monday morning.

He was a careful student of the Bible and knew how to use the original languages. "There is no short-cut to the understanding of the Word of God," he told a British Keswick congregation in 1957. "It is going to take diligence, stamina, the giving of yourself to it, if you are to know the Word of God." And, of course, it was not enough simply to study the Bible: the believer must *live* what God teaches him. In a 1970 chapel message, he warned the students of the danger of *learning* divorced from *living*.

> And that, young people, is one of the dangers in a school like Moody Bible Institute, where the teachers, having

gone on with God and laid hold of much truth from the Word of God, share it with you and feed it to you before you've had an opportunity to experience the truth of what has already been said. . . . It isn't enough to have a theoretical knowledge of the Word of God . . . if you are to be mature . . . you must also have the experience of that Word.

Dr. Culbertson had a wonderful sense of humor, but he rarely let it be seen in the pulpit. He did not criticize other men who were able to use humor in their ministry. (If that were the case, numbers of them would never have been invited to the annual Founder's Week conference.) It was simply that the emphasis of his ministry on holy living did not leave room for much laughter in the pulpit. This may have been one reason that he did not like to speak at banquets. His was the kind of preaching that demanded an expectant, hushed congregation, worshipers with open Bibles before them; and not an overfed group of "jolly good fellows" sitting around tables drinking coffee. However, his dislike for banquets stemmed from more than just the atmosphere, because he equally disliked picnics and church potluck socials. To him, it seemed utterly ridiculous to eat out in a park when a man had a comfortable kitchen and dining room at home—free from insects!

His chapel messages were usually given in series, such as the fruit of the Spirit in Galatians 5, or the exposition of a key passage of Scripture, such as 1 Corinthians 3. But occasionally, he would interrupt a series to give a special message God laid on his heart, often speaking to some particular situation confronting the school family. On October 15, 1948, he shared this burden with the students and staff.

From time to time we have spoken of our financial need. I am not sure that we have made it plain enough for all of you to share in the realization of the gravity of our condition. We are definitely at the place in which our actual cash balance for operating expenses will care for no more than the pro rate cost of running the Institute for a day or two. Just because we have money in the bank to protect our annuitants, and money that has been given designated for buildings, should not give us encouragement here. These funds, in all honesty, must be untouched. We are at the place in which we shall have to trust the Lord for our daily bread—and, judging by the past months, it will take a miracle to meet the need.

He did not use the situation to frighten them but rather to draw all of them closer to the Lord. It was not a question of raising money; it was a question of being worthy of God's supply.

Now, I am not complaining about our position; in many respects it is good for us. On the other hand, I cannot help but ask myself and you, Are we in the place in which God can, in keeping with His holiness, meet our need? We all know that God has well-defined requirements for us, if we are to know the fullness of His blessing in the supply of our daily needs. One verse is enough to prove it: "Seek ye first the kingdom of God, and his righteousness; and all these things shall be added unto you" (Mt 6:33). We must, if we are honest before God, ask ourselves the question: "Am I seeking first the kingdom of God?" All of us must face this question: trustees, administration, faculty, office workers, maintenance workers, sales staff—no one is excepted.

He never tired of reminding the students that "the future is *now*." In fact, as early as 1944, when he was serving as dean, he brought a chapel message on that very theme. "Students sometimes make the mistake of thinking that the only thing that matters is the field of service to be occupied upon graduation," he said. "This idea invariably leads to a very false conception of the period of training—the student regarding it as a hardship to be endured, or disregarding it as vital at all." This attitude can be a subtle form of procrastination, he explained, with the student forgetting that faithful study is as much a ministry in the will of God as serving on a mission station.

"Careful and thorough preparation is essential to a fruitful life of service." he stated, "so get all the training you can. What you are *today* largely determines what you will be then. Yes, we make allowances for the grace of God, the instruction of the Spirit—some changes may come. But by and large, what we have just said is true. The careless student is a careless preacher, missionary, or Christian worker. Let us be concerned about *today!*"

On occasion, the chapel service included something special for the Institute employees. On September 28, 1953, Dr. Culbertson presented service pins to several employees and took the opportunity to deal with matters relating to Christian service, a topic that was not foreign to the needs of the students. Basing his message on 1 Corinthians 12:12—13: 13, Dr. Culbertson discussed "the high and holy privilege, the deep and sacred responsibility of being in Christian work."

> God really doesn't need our service. Acts 17:25 tells us, "Neither is worshipped with men's hands, as though he needed any thing, seeing he giveth to all life, and breath, and all things." And 1 Corinthians 3:7 says, "So then neither is he that planteth any thing, neither he that watereth: but God that giveth the increase."

The important thing is to be "in the position to be used. God places us in the body of Christ, and God has placed us at Moody Bible Institute." He then gave a forty-year pin to Dr. P. B. Fitzwater, who had been a student at the Institute in Moody's day; to Miss Elizabeth Thompson, he gave a forty-five year pin; and to Miss Gertrude German he gave a fifty-five year pin. He always enjoyed these occasions, because he felt that faithful Christian service ought to be recognized, not only to the glory of God and the honor of the recipient, but also as an example for the students.

> No place is unworthy, if it be a place God has chosen. No service is mean, if it be a service to which He has called us. . . . To realize this is to take seriously and joyfully whatever our appointed work may be, knowing that, as we fulfill it, we are accomplishing His purpose; knowing also that, as we do so, we are enabling all the other members to do likewise.

Some of Dr. Culbertson's chapel notes reflect the day-to-day problems that are bound to appear when so many people live, study, and work together in the heart of a big city. One note says: "Chapel—Euphemistic expressions—Golly, Gosh, Gee, etc.—use of first names." This is written with a large hand on a large piece of paper, so it must have been important! Another memo reads: "Heb. 12:4—Resist unto blood, struggle against sin. Our effeminate age; we are listness, no moral force." In a series of messages on public prayer he gave his listeners some valuable spiritual counsel.

> Avoid whining and being doleful—the sanctimonious tone. Be natural. Avoid continuous repetition of God's name in prayer. Avoid saying "Oh, God" at the beginning and ending of each sentence. Always give thanks. Bring out the element of praise. Avoid relating past experiences in prayer; the Lord knows all about them. Beware of praising men in your prayer. Beware of hitting at others in prayer. Forget that others are around you, but most of all forget yourself.

Of course, there were always people with suggestions for chapel topics, and the president graciously received them;

but he never used the chapel pulpit to promote personal crusades. "The following are a few suggestions for topics that Dr. Culbertson might discuss during chapel hours," began a four-page memo from one of the deans, addressed to Mr. Crowell. The "few suggestions" included matters relating to time, money, and worship, to "Spearing of the bread with fork that has already been used," and "Using the spoon in the sugar bowl after it [the spoon] has been put in the mouth." There were times when the president dealt rather forcefully with matters of Christian behavior, but it was always in the context of Christian truth. On January 11, 1971, in a chapel message from Philippians 3:12-14, he had this to say:

> Don't think of these three years at Moody Bible Institute merely as preparatory. I understand in a sense they are. Get involved in this matter of utter surrender to God, this matter of meaning business with God, of pressing on in the will of God, right from the start. In the classroom, in the dormitories, in the social part of life, in your Practical Christian Work, in all of life—mean business with God. For the probability is this: that what you are at Moody Bible Institute, you'll be when you leave Moody Bible Institute. "Conformed to the image of His Son." That's the objective, and Paul says, "I press on." God help us all to press on!

He looked upon the student body as his maturing "sons and daughters," and ministered to them in love.

Two other preaching ministries should be mentioned because they were a constant source of encouragement and help to many Christians, particularly those in spiritual service. Dr. Culbertson spoke each week over the Institute radio stations in a half-hour program of a devotional nature. These messages were taped in the radio studios of WMBI at the Institute, and were released later in Chicago and other cities. While his messages were sermonic in form, the style of delivery was conversational and personal, with the kind of intensity that always marked Dr. Culbertson's ministry of the Word. His purpose was to expound the Word to help Christians grow spiritually and serve Christ better. Whatever benefits came to the work of the Institute were secondary; his first desire was to glorify Christ through the Word.

Of course, he often preached messages in series, just as he had done from the very beginning of his ministry. But he also watched the calendar and tried to schedule topics that would be timely, especially when the great Christian celebrations occured. He did not attempt to be sensational or to catch the attention of the careless unbeliever; he ministered to the concerned Christian who wanted to enter into the deeper things of the Christian life. However, he never minimized the gospel; he took every opportunity to make the way of salvation clear. For example, in his radio message for September 21, 1970, he said:

> Don't be afraid of that word *salvation*. Don't be afraid of the verb *to save*. It's a good biblical word. It means, you see, we are in danger; and the danger is not simply to drown and lose our physical life, but to go out into an eternity apart from God, and have our spirit separated from the Lord forever! And that, believe you me, is real danger.

A statement like "believe you me" did not often appear in a Culbertson sermon! It only indicates, however, the depth of his feeling as he tried to explain to the lost sinner the meaning of judgment and of salvation.

"Man to Man" was the second preaching ministry that must be noted, not only for its practical content, but also for its unique outreach. "Man to Man" was a series of 45 rpm recordings that Dr. Culbertson made especially for pastors and other Christian workers. He began the series in 1962 and continued it through 1970, and in each recording, he sought to apply the Word of God to the work of the ministry. William Culbertson was at his best when preaching to preachers, and "Man to Man" was no exception.

> My brother in the ministry, it is a great privilege which is mine to have the opportunity to speak to you once again. The high calling which is ours in Christ Jesus is surely a priceless privilege. But, like all privileges, it carries with it great responsibility. The possibility of tragedy is always before us.

So begins record number seventeen, "The Pastor's Heart." It continues with a quotation from an old hymn from *The Olney Hymnal*:

> When Contradictions meet
>   In ministers' employ,
> It is a bitter sweet,
>   A sorrow full of joy;
> No other post affords a place
> For equal honor or disgrace.

> If you and I are going to escape the peril, we shall have to give attention to our hearts. A preacher of the Old Testament said, "Keep thy heart with all diligence; for out of it are the issues of life" (Pr 4:23). . . . How is it with your heart?

He then gives what he believes are the "ingredients of a heart that is rich toward God": consecration to God's will, a consistent devotional life, and tenderness toward others. He quotes an interesting statement from his highly-esteemed G. Campbell Morgan, that perhaps is more applicable today than when Dr. Morgan said it and Dr. Culbertson quoted it:

"The study of the Bible will curse us in the next ten years if we are not careful" [said Morgan]. Men will tabulate and analyze and think they know everything. Man, listen, for unless as the result of your study of the Bible you hear the imperial tone, the voice of the living Christ talking in your inmost soul, your Bible knowledge is mere technique that will burn you and ruin you in the next ten years.

The sequel to "The Pastor's Heart" was "The Pastor's Mind," and here he unburdened himself concerning the preparation of messages.

May God deliver us from shoddy preparation! For surely it is inexcusable to attempt to speak for God without having let God speak to us. He will speak to us carefully and help us to communicate what He has said in an intelligent, logical, and spiritual manner. It is perfectly evident that pietistic speech is not enough. Actually, pious phrases may needlessly drive men away from the Lord and His message. . . . There is a balance that is to be sought and found, a balance between spirituality and scholarship. Dr. Jowett has said, "Preaching that costs nothing accomplishes nothing. If the study is a lounge, the pulpit will be an impertinence."

What must the pastor do? "Be most careful in the use of our time in the study," Dr. Culbertson advises.

Be very careful that truth is digested. Don't jump too quickly to preach on a text or theme. Let it soak in; let it begin to live. Be willing to say, "It is not ready yet." Normally, to be ready to speak on anything at the drop of a hat is a sign of shallowness, not profundity. . . . In all your getting of knowledge, make sure that whatever God is saying touches you and reaches you where you live.

These messages were not "ground out" in academic fashion; they were the overflow of William Culbertson's heart, as he carried on his own ministry and sought to share the burdens of many others in the ministry. In record number nine, he said,

> Brother in Christ, fellow servant of our Lord, there is a burden on my heart. Forgive me if I seem blunt. I can only say that God in recent days has been talking to me plainly, pointedly, and powerfully. Perhaps He wants to say something to you of what He is saying to me. Because I know your heart, because I know something of the perils which beset you, I am emboldened to speak. What I say comes from a heart of love, and with earnest prayer on your behalf. May God make us the men of God we must be if our lives are to count for God.

The burden of his message was that God's servants (himself included) have a "divine discontent"—a desire to see "more of God, more of God's working . . . more heavenly power . . . more of a crashing through the superficiality of playing religion, to virile, vibrant, victorious Christianity." He quotes one of his favorite authors, Bishop J. C. Ryle, who writes in his book *Holiness*: "It is terribly possible to live a careless, easy-going, half-worldly life, and yet at the same time to maintain evangelical principles, and call ourselves evangelical people." Then he says,

> May God bring us to the place where we are desperate enough to be afraid of anything less than to be sold out to God. I have no way of knowing just what it is God will say to you in the light of this Word which He has said to me. I recognize my obligation to Him at least in measure. With God's help, I am going to go on with Him. May God lead you and the work He has given you, in such a way that you will not be ashamed at the judgment seat of Christ.

No one really knows how many discouraged Christians were encouraged to stay with their ministry because they heard one or more of the "Man to Man" records. Perhaps it came as a surprise to some that the president of the Moody Bible Institute could understand their heart's needs so precisely. After all, was he not a busy academic leader in a secluded office on the ninth floor of Crowell Hall? Yes, he was; but he was also—and always would be—"the bishop," the man with a pastor's heart.

*"Churches are not to be held together
except by an instructive ministry; a
mere filling up of time with oratory
will not suffice. Everywhere men have
to be fed, really fed."*

"Man to Man"

TEN

The Wider Ministry

When William Culbertson became president of the Moody
Bible Institute, he not only retained his bishop's office, but
he also retained a bishop's heart. He had a deep love for
Christians in general, and for pastors and Christian workers
in particular. To many, he was "a pastor's pastor." The
announcement that Dr. Culbertson was addressing a conference would usually bring to the meeting pastors from
miles around, because they knew they would be fed and
encouraged in the work of the ministry.

His summers were largely devoted to conference ministry,
including the weeks he and the family spent at the Island
Grove Camp Meeting at Mexico, Pennsylvania, their favorite
vacation spot. During the school year, he selected those
preaching engagements that he felt warranted his being
away from the campus. Whenever he left on an extended
itinerary, Miss Hogan would usually give him a schedule of
dates and places (and driving instructions, if necessary);
and often Dr. Culbertson would keep the record of his messages on that schedule.

It is interesting to go through his preaching file, if only to discover how often he preached (sometimes three times a day) and how varied were the topics that he used. To be sure, there were some messages that he repeated often, not because he was low on ammunition, but because God had singularly blessed those messages and they were worth repeating. "When God Sings" was a favorite, as was also "The Work of the Holy Spirit" and "Christ in You." But he did not carry with him the traditional homiletical "barrel" and turn it over when he arrived in a new situation. He constantly sought the mind of the Lord in selecting messages, and tried not to permit any message to become routine. He lived in the Word, and the Word lived in him; and this meant a fresh supply of truth to share with his congregations.

The "round robin" conferences were the most difficult. These he shared with two or three other preachers, and the men would be in different churches each night of the week and sometimes there were morning meetings. Often, there would also be a Moody alumni meeting to address, and perhaps a special pastors' session. Between sessions, he would try to keep up with his academic responsibilities, but he tried not to miss any meetings, even when he was not the preacher. "I need to hear other men," he admitted, "and I need to sense the way the Spirit is working. Besides, it's an insult to my fellow speakers if I ignore them."

During the 1948 Prophetic Conference in New York City, Dr. Culbertson spoke thirteen times in five different locations over a period of eight days. His sermon topics are written on the schedule in his minuscule fashion: "The Practical Meaning of Prophecy," "Three Requirements for Discipleship," "God's Grace — Titus 2:11-13," "Perfect Peace — Isa. 26:3-4," and the references to an exposition of Ephesians 1.

During his 1951 Northwest conference in Seattle and Ta-

coma, he even had sessions at seven o'clock in the morning!
What did he serve the saints at that early hour? "Five Basic
Truths from Romans"! On successive mornings, they heard
him teach what Paul wrote about guilt, propitiation, as-
surance, victory, and Christian liberty. Most men would
have avoided serving spiritual meat for breakfast, but not
William Culbertson. He was convinced that meat was ex-
actly what the saints needed, and that any man who would
come out to an early morning Bible study must have a good
appetite!

When he remained at one center for a conference, he
usually brought a series of messages. A schedule from his
1952 Florida ministry reveals that he preached a morning
series on the great doctrines of the faith, and an evening
series on "Questions God Asks." Six questions are listed,
beginning with, "Where art thou?," and ending with, "Why
do the heathen rage?" Interestingly enough, on this same
schedule is a listing of the attendance figures at the various
meetings.

Dr. Culbertson often teamed up with other Moody staff
members in areawide round robin conferences. In 1955,
he ministered with Donald P. Hustad, then director of the
department of sacred music, and Clayton Halvorson, member of the music faculty. The three men visited key churches
in Oklahoma, Texas, Arkansas, and Tennessee, in ten days
of whirlwind activity. Dr. Culbertson was scheduled to
preach ten times, but after the schedule was printed, four
more meetings were added.

He and Don Hustad were often paired for the wider ministries of the Institute, and a happy pairing it was. Dr. Culbertson loved good church music and was especially fond of
the liturgy of the Reformed Episcopal Church. He knew the
great hymns of the church and was able to name his favorite hymn tunes from memory. He had a warm appreciation
for Mr. Hustad's ministry with the Moody Chorale, and he

knew that the music at the meeting would beautifully complement the message from the Word. Mr. Hustad recalls:

> Dr. Culbertson was also a connoisseur of good food and good restaurants. I believe that in his early student days, he once worked in a grocery store, and this may have added to his gourmet knowledge. When we participated in conferences in churches in the east, he was always ready to suggest what he considered to be the best restaurant in the area.
>
> I remember when we were in a conference at Park Street Church in Boston one time, we set out for Durgin Park Restaurant, which is located in the market area. On the way, he mentioned that Durgin Park was not especially noted for lobster but that the other food was excellent. After we had all ordered other food, Dr. Culbertson ordered—yes, you guessed it—lobster! It turned out to be about the biggest and best one that we had ever seen! I never quite figured out whether he was trying to safeguard our waistlines or what, but we never let him forget his treachery.

It is worth noting that it was Dr. Culbertson who urged Mr. Hustad to compose a new tune for George Matheson's "Make Me A Captive, Lord," one of his favorites.

To leaf through Dr. Culbertson's preaching file is to travel by imagination to the great conferences and preaching centers of the United States and Canada: Winona Lake; Mt. Hermon; Hume Lake; Maranatha; American Keswick; Word of Life at Schroon Lake, New York; Forest Home; Cannon Beach, Oregon; Sandy Cove, Maryland; Montrose, Pennsylvania; and many more. It also brings to mind many of the great preachers of that era with whom he often ministered; many of whom are now home with the Lord.

Most people who heard him preach identified him as a "deeper life preacher," and to a great degree they were correct. Dr. Culbertson emphasized victory over sin through the power of the Spirit, and growth in practical holiness; but he did not make a habit of the "victorious Christian life" theme. Nor did he attempt to give people the idea that one step would solve all their problems. His messages were extremely practical, beaten out on the anvil of experience and not manufactured in the isolation of some comfortable ivory tower.

He ministered at British Keswick in 1954, 1957, 1967, and 1971; and he also ministered at Irish Keswick in 1967 and 1971. Located in the beautiful Lake district of England, the little town of Keswick has been the location for this "conference for the deepening of the Christian life" since 1875. To read its history is to read the roll of some of the most gifted preachers in British church history: the list includes J. Elder Cumming, Northcote Deck, W. Y. Fullerton, S. D. Gordon, Evan Hopkins, John McNeill, Gregory Mantle, F. B. Meyer, G. Campbell Morgan, A. T. Pierson, W. Graham Scroggie, and Andrew Murray. Not many American preachers have ministered there: among them are Wilbur M. Smith, Donald Barnhouse, Paul Rees, and William Culbertson. Interdenominational in its outreach and biblical in its emphasis, British Keswick has been a vibrant center for "the deeper Christian life" for nearly a century.

Dr. Culbertson's first message was at the three o'clock meeting on Monday, July 19, 1954; and he spoke on "The Christian's Attitude Toward Sin," taking Psalm 97:10 and Romans 12:9 as his texts. It is traditional at the Keswick conference to emphasize "the sinfulness of sin" on Monday, and then during the week to bring out the biblical steps for dealing with sin and entering into a sincere dedication experience with the Lord. The next evening, he spoke from Psalm 27:1, "My Light, and Salvation, and Strength." It was a dramatic message on the power of Christ to set the defeated Christian free from the bondage of sin.

Oh, dear heart, the glory of Christianity is this—Christ liveth in me! Oh, believe it! Believe it! It is the Word of God. It is no longer I that live, but "Christ liveth in me."

Christianity is nothing if it is not supernatural. If there is not a living Christ, who comes to live in us, we may as well throw out the Word of God as a fabrication of lies, and the whole story of the gospel as a hoax. But, it is true! It is gloriously true!

In the next two messages, he dealt with "The Conditions of Discipleship" and "The Ministry of the Spirit in Us," two of his favorite themes.

His series in 1957 was so singularly used of God that it later appeared in the only book Dr. Culbertson published during his lifetime, *God's Provision for Holy Living*. These "Bible Readings" (as the British term them) explain the "spiritual heritage of God's children" that can be used to make the believer more and more like Christ. In his foreword, Keswick convention chairman Rev. A. T. Houghton, says: "For anyone who was privileged to hear the author as morning by morning he unfolded his theme of God's provision for holy living, it may be possible to recapture the intonation of his voice as with the deepest sincerity he gripped his audience with the proclamation of the glorious inheritance of the people of God."

He spoke at four convention meetings in 1967, which was held from July 15 to July 21. Following the meetings, he went to London and preached at Westminster Chapel, Buckingham Gate, the church made famous by the ministries of G. Campbell Morgan and D. Martyn Lloyd-Jones. Dr. Culbertson had long been an admirer of Morgan's ministry, and having the privilege of preaching from his pulpit—and of wearing Morgan's pulpit gown—was a great experience for him. His sermons the first Sunday were "What Happened at Calvary" and "Why the Lord Died." On July 30, he preached on "If Need Be" and "When God Sings."

Dr. and Mrs. Culbertson always enjoyed ministering in Great Britain. To be sure, his own family came from Scotland and Ireland; but even more than the natural ties were the spiritual bonds that drew them to those of like faith in the Keswick fellowship, both the British and the North of Ireland conventions.

The 1971 trip to both conventions was born out of two letters Dr. Culbertson wrote on January 23, 1969, one to Canon A. T. Houghton of the British Keswick Convention, and the other to James McDonald in Belfast. He had recently had lunch with Alan Redpath and George Duncan, both well-known Keswick speakers, and the possibility of a 1971 trip was discussed. In connection with this conversation, Dr. Culbertson had been conferring with his associates at the Institute regarding his plans for the summer of 1971. He wrote to Canon Houghton,

> My colleagues and I have been prayerfully looking to the Lord concerning my summer ministry. As it looks now, this year I shall largely be in California. In 1970, the Lord willing, it will be in the eastern part of the United States and in Canada. Our thought is to explore the possibility of a return trip to Great Britain in June and July of 1971. . . . I know that the Keswick Convention is in no need of another American voice, and that the program must be put together with men the Lord leads the Council to invite, but I do not want to omit letting you know of this possibility —with the understanding that however the Lord leads, I shall understand.

Of course, both conventions were delighted that the bishop was available, and he was scheduled to speak at British Keswick July 9-17, and at Portstewart, Northern Ireland, June 19-28, with other preaching engagements and opportunities for "rest and recuperation" added to the schedule. The Culbertsons' close friend, Dr. Alan Redpath, formerly pastor of the Moody Memorial Church and now associated with the Capernwray Fellowship, helped to arrange the itinerary. He insisted that his friends take time to enjoy the beauties of Great Britain and not spend the entire trip in a busy preaching ministry. His suggestion turned out to be a wise one, because on June 4, 1970, while the Institute was engaged in commencement activities, Dr. Culbertson underwent serious lung surgery for cancer at Chicago's Swedish Covenant Hospital. He was forced to cancel all of his 1970 summer engagements, but the doctor did permit him to make his trip abroad the next year. It was to be his final visit to places that he dearly loved and with friends who had enriched his own life and ministry.

He and Mrs. Culbertson left Chicago's O'Hare Airport at midnight, June 14, arriving in London the next afternoon. They caught a flight to Belfast, arriving in the late afternoon; and there, they rented a car and spent four leisurely days at Port Ballintree, then driving to Portstewart on Saturday. Dr. Culbertson shared the opening meeting on Saturday evening with Dr. James Dunlop; and the next morning, he preached at the local Methodist church. Monday through Thursday, at 10:30 each morning, he gave the Bible Readings, dealing with "the natural man, the carnal Christian, and the spiritual Christian." He also spoke Thursday evening, Friday morning at a prayer session, and twice on Sunday.

They drove to the Belfast airport on Monday morning, June 28, and took a plane to Glasgow, where they rented another car and spent the next eleven days touring Scotland. What a glorious trip it was! Here was the land of Bonar and McCheyne, Rutherford and Alexander Whyte! It was here that his theological roots were deeply planted, and he rejoiced that the Lord had privileged him to make the pilgrimage.

He spoke four times at British Keswick, twice on Sunday in area churches, and on Monday morning and Thursday evening in "the big tent." His two messages were "Righteous Lot" and "The Holy Spirit—a Blessed Person," and together they perfectly summarized all he had been teaching and preaching for nearly fifty years—separation from the world and the fullness of the Holy Spirit. After a few days with Dr. Redpath at Capernwray, and a brief visit to London, Dr. and Mrs. Culbertson left for home, arriving at O'Hare Thursday afternoon, July 22.

               ❂   ❂   ❂

But his wider ministry took him much farther than this, for William Culbertson had a passion for missions. He told the 1958 Founder's Week congregation:

> I'll be frank with you. One of the reasons I came to Moody Bible Institute was that under God and with His blessing, I felt I could have a bigger part in the march of missions to the ends of the earth by touching young people. That's the only reason I gave up the position I had in the East. I'm here because I believe God is doing something and I want to be in the march.

Dr. Culbertson enjoyed *being* places, but he was not enthusiastic about *going* places. He was a patient traveller, always happy to arrive! "My wife will travel at the drop of a hat," he would tell people, and yet he made three trips to the mission field and five to the Holy Land. He especially enjoyed ocean travel, particularly on the *Queen Mary* and the *Queen Elizabeth I*. He feared he would get seasick, but he never did, and he delighted in the relaxation he could experience aboard ship.

In 1952, he made a seven-week tour of the Near and Middle East accompanied by Dr. Irwin Moon, director of the

Moody Institute of Science. They made Beirut, Lebanon, their headquarters, and visited Iraq, Iran, Jordan, Israel, Syria, and Egypt, looking for material they could use in future films. Dr. Culbertson had hoped to do a film on Bible geography—his favorite subject—but circumstances made it impossible. "While in the countries visited," he told the Institute family, "I felt the presence of the devil, the bondage of Satan, and the enslavement of human souls as never before." Of course, the inroads of Communism and the tensions between Jews and Arabs disturbed him.

"Did you come back depressed by all you've seen?" a reporter asked him; and he replied, "I came back tremendously challenged. No, not depressed. There is power in the gospel to meet the need of the hardest heart. But the job calls for more power than I ever before realized."

He recalled that 1952 visit to the Holy Land in the message he gave at the 1963 Founder's Week conference:

> It was my privilege in 1952 to stand on the slope of Gordon's Calvary outside the Damascus Gate of Old Jerusalem. . . . I remember I sought out the place where a cross could stand, and I stood there visibly moved. I bowed my head, and the tears coursed down my cheeks. He loved me. He gave Himself for me.

At the request of several mission boards, Dr. Culbertson visited the fields in Africa in 1957. One of the happiest things about the trip was the fact that Harold Cook, director of the Institute's missions course, accompanied him on much of the journey. Cook was making the trip particularly to update his knowledge of the work in Africa. He left for the continent early in January, and Dr. Culbertson joined him on February 16 at Rethy in the Congo. Here, they were guests of the Africa Inland Mission for an eight-day conference centering on the second coming of Jesus Christ. Dr. Culbertson spoke both Sundays and also each morning. The daily program began with a prayer meeting at 6:15 A.M., and at the close of each evening session, Dr. Culbertson shared "a brief devotional thought."

Missionaries were there from the Congo, French East Africa, and Uganda; and many of them were Moody graduates. Mr. Cook left in the middle of the week so he could visit as many mission stations as possible, planning to meet Dr. Culbertson at Kyobe on February 25. The Culbertson party was delayed in their overland trip, so Mr. Cook substituted for the bishop and gave the opening address and also the message the following morning. Dr. Culbertson arrived to preach each morning, Wednesday through Saturday, and also at the Sunday afternoon service.

The bishop and Mr. Cook met each other on March 6 at the Nairobi airport, and Mr. Cook noticed that his companion was quite sunburned. In helping to dedicate the new A.I.M. press building at Kyobe, Dr. Culbertson had stood out in the hot African sun, and was suffering the consequences, but was not complaining. Dr. Culbertson flew to Ethiopia where he had hoped to have an audience with the emperor; but these plans fell through. On March 10, the two travellers joined forces again in Salisbury, and from that point on, remained together, visiting the Bible school at Kapjundi, the Union Bible Institute in Sweetwaters, and various ministries in Johannesburg and Durban, including meetings with Moody alumni.

"He would preach as often as three times a day," Mr. Cook recalls, "and sometimes even more. Yet each message was fresh and helpful. In Leopoldville, after preaching the same sermon for the third time on the trip, he apologized to me! I told him that I got a greater blessing out of it every time I heard it. His ministry to ministers and missionaries alike was greatly appreciated. There were times when our plane reservations were fouled up and we had long waits in uncomfortable places, but he never complained. He was a perfect travelling companion."

On March 18, they had a stormy flight from Leopoldville to Kano; but the trip was forgotten as they enjoyed a happy Moody reunion banquet with the missionaries there. The next day, they flew to Jos, where Dr. Culbertson ministered for three days. He made a quick visit to the Kent Academy at Miango where 150 missionary kids were chattering over a lunch of meat, potatoes, and the inevitable tough green peas. One of the missionaries, Mrs. Paul Craig, remembers the scene:

> A tall man in shirtsleeves stepped in out of the Nigerian sun. As he stood there in the doorway, chatting with his Sudan Interior Mission companion, he just beamed at the young people. I recognized him immediately, and Paul and I stepped to the door to greet him. He asked a number of questions about the work at Kent Academy. He had to return to Jos for the evening meeting, so we didn't spend too much time together; but those brief minutes will never be forgotten.

About sixty-five were present at Jos for the second Moody alumni banquet on March 21. The next day, the two men returned to Kano, where forty-four alumni met with the president. It was a stirring experience for Dr. Culbertson to sing the Moody "Christian Fellowship Song" with that stalwart group of missionaries so far from the city of Chicago. Both Dr. Culbertson and Mr. Cook spoke at the conference in Kano; and then on March 25, they flew to London "weary but blessed."

"Two single missionary ladies took us to the airport," Mr. Cook reports. "One of the ladies gave me an envelope and told me not to open it until we were aloft. When I opened it, I discovered a letter of appreciation that read almost like a love letter! We were so impressed that we shared it with the faculty when we arrived home."

The trip deepened Dr. Culbertson's burden for missions as well as his appreciation for missionaries and their work. He wrote in a *Moody Monthly* editorial:

> The Moody Bible Institute believes in missions. We attempt to inculcate in our students the necessity of looking to God for His will for them, particularly as to whether God wants them on the mission field. We attempt to show them, not only their duty, but their privilege in praying and giving for missions. Over three thousand former students have gone to the foreign field. Recent years have seen our students giving to the missionary enterprises well over $10,000 a year from their earnings.

> The work of world evangelism must be our passionate, our supreme interest. May we enter all the doors of opportunity! But we cannot, unless we give sacrificially, unless we pray importunately. The Christian Church has opportunities now, the like of which she has never had. Let us enter in!

During September and October 1960, Dr. Culbertson visited mission stations of The Evangelical Alliance Mission (TEAM) on fields in the Far East. The dog-eared schedule, written in his own hand, indicates that he spoke nearly one hundred times during the trip, not only to missionaries but also to church congregations and various educational institutions. His ministry began at the Chinese Christian Church of Honolulu, where he spoke Sunday, September 4, on one of his favorite subjects—"God's Peace." The next day, he addressed an alumni meeting. He flew to Korea, and on Thursday spoke from Psalm 119:11 at a TEAM orphanage in Busan. Later ministries took him to Japan, Hong Kong, the Philippines, New Guinea, Australia, Thailand, Singapore, and India. It was a long, difficult trip;

many of his messages required an interpreter; but the Lord blessed the Word wherever he went.

In his office at the Institute, there hung a picture that was given to Dr. Culbertson by his predecessor, Dr. Will Houghton. It had been given to Dr. Houghton by Dr. Charles Ernest Scott, father of Betty Scott Stam. Dr. Culbertson had known the Scotts and the Stams from his days at Ventnor, and the Church of the Atonement in Germantown was near the Doane Memorial Mission homes of the China Inland Mission. The picture was that of a simple Oriental bridge over a stream, surrounded by trees. It was significant because near that bridge, John and Betty Stam were martyred in 1934. Dr. Culbertson told a Mid-America Keswick audience at Moody Church, Chicago, on October 16, 1959,

> This poor sinner often goes over to that picture and looks at it. He cries out to God, "Oh, that I would know the mind of Christ—to give up the best, to accept the worst, to be willing to die!"

Nobody at the Moody Bible Institute ever saw their president talking to God before that simple picture, but they did see the results of his devotion. He came to the Institute to be a part of "the march of missions to the ends of the earth," and God fulfilled his desires.

"Is not your heart moved by the fact that according to the Word of God, this nation [Israel] this people, stand first to hear the judgment of God in condemnation—unless they individually and personally turn to the Saviour?"

20th Annual Conference on Prophecy and the Jew, 1964 Winona Lake, Indiana

ELEVEN

Missionary Statesman

Many Bible students have an interest in prophecy that is purely academic, but this was not true of William Culbertson. He was not satisfied to expound prophecy and then neglect people: he sought to let the prophetic Word motivate his own ministry to others. "If I were to sum up our responsibility as Christians in the present hour," he said at the Second International Conference on Prophecy in New York, 1955, "it would be in these words: *believe—stand —live—pray—work—win.*" He had no time for the Bible student who was "curious about prophecy." He believed that God revealed the future so that men might know better how to live and serve in the present.

One of his great concerns was the work of Jewish evangelism, a concern he had even in his early pastoral ministry. He often invited missionaries to the Jews to speak in his churches and was anxious to cooperate with local evangeli-

cal witnesses to Israel. In his prophetic messages, he underscored the importance of Jewish evangelism, and he op-
posed anti-Semitism with a vigor that seemed almost foreign
to his nature. And so it was not surprising that in September
1948, Dr. Culbertson accepted the invitation from Dr. J. Palmer Muntz to serve on the advisory board of the American
Association for Jewish Evangelism.

Actually, Dr. Muntz extended two invitations in the same
letter: to serve on the AAJE board, and also to become a
member of the Winona Lake Bible Conference Committee,
of which Dr. Muntz was the director. Dr. Culbertson considered the matter prayerfully and discussed it with his
trustees (he had been president of the school only eight
months); and together, they decided that the AAJE ministry was the one God would have him accept. He wrote to
Dr. Muntz:

> You will remember that I indicated to you something of
> the problem that we have in that we want to be sparing in
> the use of our name and we do want to be more than just
> a nominal member of a committee. It has become in-
> creasingly clear as the Lord's will that I ought to say "yes"
> to the invitation to participate in the limited measure in-
> volved in the American Association for Jewish Evangelism
> and "no" to the gracious invitation to become a member of
> the Winona Conference Committee.

Eight years later, Dr. Muntz telephoned Dr. Culbertson to
ask him to consider once again serving on the conference
committee. The president told him that it was a matter on
which he could not give an immediate answer, but that he
would discuss it with his fellow workers and make it a matter of prayer. A few days later, he wrote,

> Despite my very real love for the work of Winona and my
> very real affection for you, I must say that I sense no con-
> firmation from the Lord that I should accept the election to

the Board of Winona. I suppose this particular conviction grows out of a sense that there is only so much that I can do and do with some small degree of creditability. Frankly, with what I have before me at the Institute and the responsibilities which I have already assumed so far as other organizations are concerned, it is not the part of wisdom to attempt more.

In a day when it is easy for a Christian leader to belong to a committee with which he never meets, endorsing a ministry about which he knows next to nothing, Dr. Culbertson's decision has to be admired. He felt that there were others who could do a better job of helping to guide the conference than he could; but when it came to reaching the Jew for Christ, this struck a responsive note in his heart.

He was made the chairman of the advisory council, serving with Dr. Hyman Appleman, chairman of the executive board; but in actual practice, after a few years, Dr. Culbertson led the board meetings even when the president was present. Later, Dr. Muntz replaced Dr. Appleman. Had the two men not been very close friends, Dr. Culbertson would never have agreed to such an arrangement; but over the years, their friendship deepened, and working together was a constant delight. So sensitive was Dr. Culbertson to any abuse of office or authority, that he even complained about the placing of his name in one of the AAJE advertisements in *Moody Monthly*. On June 2, 1949, he wrote to the noted evangelist, Dr. Hyman Appleman:

> I noticed in the June issue of *Moody Monthly*, page 730, the advertisement of the American Association for Jewish Evangelism in which my name is placed before yours, and the indication is that I am chairman of the Board.
>
> Of course, I am glad to have my name associated with this work, and I rejoice in the blessing of God upon it. On the other hand, I cannot help but feel that the prominence

given my name, and the designation, is such as to cause people to come to an erroneous conclusion. In any case, it does seem wise, if my name is to be used at all, that I be designated as chairman of the Advisory Council rather than as chairman of the Board, since the latter designation, in many corporations, indicates a tremendously important position. You understand that I do not look upon the position as chairman of the Advisory Council as unimportant, but simply as relatively in second place to that of the actual Board.

Dr. A. B. Machlin was the general director of the AAJE ministry, and he and Dr. Culbertson worked together to strengthen the ministry and extend its important influence. On July 27, 1960, when Mrs. Machlin died, Dr. Culbertson wrote one of his typically compassionate letters of sympathy to his friend and fellow worker.

Today a faithful loving handmaid of the Lord went triumphantly into His presence. Today, in the presence of our Heavenly Father, Who is all-wise and cannot make a mistake, and Who is all-love and cannot be cruel to any of His children, your help-meet of the years, your beloved Edna has gone on ahead. Oh, how you will miss her! How we all shall miss her! She was not only all that a wife could be, she gave unstinted service, selfless devotion and gracious ministry for the work of the Association. Comparatively few could know of her major contribution to Jewish Evangelism. She said nothing of herself. Only by being present, by seeing something of the day-by-day work of this servant of God could you begin to detect the largeness of her ministry.

Not content with simply writing one letter of condolence, Dr. Culbertson wrote him again on August 10 and included a contribution toward the Edna Machlin Memorial Fund. "She was a wonderful friend to Mrs. Culbertson and me and the children—one in a million. We look forward to the day when we shall forever be with the Lord!"

In 1962, Dr. Machlin was called home, and the pastor of Chicago's Northwest Baptist Church, Ralph Gade, was named executive director. The office was moved from Winona Lake, Indiana, to Chicago, making it even more convenient for Dr. Culbertson to meet with the people who were involved in the ministry. He tried to arrange his summer schedule so that he might participate in the annual AAJE conference at Winona Lake, sharing the ministry with men who, like him, had a heart for reaching both Jews and Gentiles for Christ.

Dr. Culbertson made his second trip to the Holy Land in 1961, this time under the auspices of AAJE. The 1961 AAJE group left New York on the *Queen Mary* April 5, and Dr. Culbertson spoke each day they were at sea. On Thursday, Friday, and Saturday, he dealt with his favorite theme—the geography and history of ancient kingdoms. He spoke at both the morning and evening services on Sunday; and during the group's stay in London, he addressed them on various prophetic themes. After their arrival in the Holy Land, he delighted in both the geographical and prophetical truths that he could share with them. The *Jerusalem Times* published a photo of the group, with the appropriate quotation, "We are delighted to be again in Jordan, under the distinguished leadership of King Hussein and appreciate the graciousness with which we have been received."

The third AAJE tour, in 1964, was in cooperation with the Moody Alumni Association, and Dr. Lehman Strauss joined the preaching staff to assist Ralph Gade, Palmer Muntz, and Dr. Culbertson. They embarked on the *Queen Elizabeth* on Thursday, April 2, and arrived in Southampton on Tuesday, April 7. During the crossing, Dr. Culbertson repeated his series on "The Locale and Power of Ancient Kingdoms," and Dr. Muntz gave illustrated lectures on the

Holy Land. After the usual tours of London, the group flew on to Paris, Rome, Cairo, and Damascus, finally arriving at Jerusalem on April 22. They returned to New York on May 8. During the trip, Dr. Culbertson kept the record of his messages on the tour schedule and this time included several words in Hebrew!

During these years of association with AAJE, Dr. Culbertson and Dr. Muntz became fast friends. They joined forces again in the spring of 1966 for the Holy Land tour, and then that fall, Dr. Culbertson asked Dr. Muntz to be his roommate when they both went to Berlin for the World Congress on Evangelism. The two friends rooming together was certainly of the Lord, because at 4 A.M. November 2, Dr. Culbertson answered the phone in their room to receive the message that Mrs. Palmer Muntz had suddenly passed away.

"The news came with a sense of shock," Dr. Muntz recalled, "and yet a consciousness of our great God's presence, sustaining grace, and the realization that 'He hath done all things well.' Rather numbly, I went about the task of packing and how glad I was for, and strengthened by, the companionship of my beloved friend whom I have been privileged for years to call 'Bill.' "

Knowing so well Dr. Culbertson's concern in these matters, his secretary, May Hogan, made plane reservations for the Culbertsons; and when the president arrived back in Chicago late Saturday night, he was prepared to leave Sunday morning for Buffalo, New York. Of course, it was only right that he bring a message at the three o'clock memorial service. He spoke from Psalm 127:2—"For so he giveth his beloved sleep."

The 1969 tour was Dr. Culbertson's last trip to the Holy Land, and once again, his wife went along. The Chicago *Sun-Times* for May 3 published a picture of the Culbertsons standing by some of the ruins at Jerusalem. It was during that trip that Dr. and Mrs. Ralph Gade and the Culbertsons were privileged to have an audience with David Ben-Gurion. It was more than the usual formal visit, because the men had the opportunity of discussing the Christian faith with the Jewish leader. In a letter of appreciation to Mr. Ben-Gurion, Dr. Culbertson wrote,

> During the course of our conversation I was aware, of course, of your position relative to the relationship of Paul and the Lord Jesus. I know that you are aware that there is another position than that current Christianity, at least in doctrinal content, is Paulinism rather than Christian. Without thought of being controversial, I felt you would be glad to see a scholarly work on the matter from the position of those of us who are conservative in our theology. For that reason, I am taking the liberty of sending you a copy of "The Origin of Paul's Religion" by Dr. J. Gresham Machen.
>
> Our visit to Israel was very wonderful. I continue to marvel at the initiative, the industry and the utter devotion of the people to the work of rebuilding Israel. It is a source of inspiration indeed. Some of us, of course, believe that this could well be the prelude to what the Old Testament prophets predicted. You manifested such a complete grasp of the religious side of the matter that I am sure you know that some of us do believe in a personal Messiah and that there are days of great glory awaiting your nation.

"It is apparent that the family life of the pastor should be exemplary. Indeed, the home should provide the happiest of atmospheres if a man is to be used of God to the extent that the Lord wants to use him."

"Man to Man"

TWELVE

The Head of the Home

When her father was elected president of Moody Bible Institute, Joy Anne Culbertson was nearly eighteen and about to graduate from high school. She entered Wheaton College, Wheaton, Illinois, that September, and the following year, her father was invited to lead the annual evangelistic meeting on campus. The student newspaper, *The Wheaton Record*, took advantage of her presence to get an exclusive article describing the homelife of their esteemed guest speaker, and her father. She wrote:

> I have been asked to write a composition on my father, Dr. William Culbertson, who will lead the evangelistic services next week.
>
> My father was a remarkably good child. At an early age he shot off the balls from the Christmas tree with his pop gun, and I think this is why none of us children was ever allowed to have a gun.

129

At fourteen he was hit by a car, his hair turned curly, and he entered West Philadelphia High. After graduation from West Philly and the Reformed Episcopal Seminary he married my mother. That she, like father, has no brothers or sisters particularly distresses me on my birthday.

Before moving to Evanston in 1942, my father had pastorates in Collingdale, Pa., Ventnor, N.J., and Philadelphia, and also attended Temple University.

My father's favorite saying is, "Look it up in the dictionary!" When a word is looked up in Webster, he claims, it will stick in one's mind much longer than if he had told the meaning. We children have another explanation, however.

If he has one particular hobby, I suppose it is fishing. My father is a REAL fisherman because [he goes] where there aren't many fish. Thus it is a major victory when he catches several fish in one evening.

Father is also an amateur gardener. Ever since the era of victory gardens, the center of our yard has been taken up with Father's plot. Despite my brothers' ball-playing and numerous dogs, the patch has usually fared quite well, except for the strawberries. For three years or so, my father has worked over a strawberry bed. Each year when the fruit is ready to bear, however, we leave on our vacation.

His favorite possessions are his fishing pants, tennis hat, and an ancient bathing suit, which soon will be eaten by moths, I hope.

Seriously, though, I am really proud of my father. He lives at home what he preaches at church and is to me what a Christian should be—not a long-faced person, but one who is able to enjoy life much more because he is a Christian.

Proof that Dr. and Mrs. Culbertson did practice what they preached is the way God has guided and used their children. Joy married Dr. Charles Huttar, who teaches at Hope College, Holland, Michigan. Both Robert and Paul are ordained ministers, and Ruth is married to Arvid Bush, who is on the Institute staff, working in the computer programming department. All of the Culbertson children except Ruth graduated from Wheaton College, but Ruth decided to attend the Institute, "even if the president *is* my father."

Dr. Culbertson loved his family and enjoyed his home. For several years, the family included Mrs. Lydia Culbertson, his mother, whom he tenderly cared for as an only son would do. In May, 1956, Mother Culbertson suffered a stroke, and after a few days, went to be with the Lord. The bishop accompanied her coffin on the train trip to Philadelphia, and Paul asked if he might go along, a request that pleased his father. Paul comments on the trip,

> When we got back to Philadelphia, Dr. Bustard lent my father his car; and for the rest of the day, my dad took me on a tour to the places he remembered as a boy. He showed me a couple of places where he had lived, a church he had gone to, a store he had gone to as a lad. He also took me to the last house his mother had owned. . . . I felt very close to my dad that day, because I knew he was sharing with me *himself*. I suppose in some ways I didn't fully understand what my dad was doing with me that day until after he himself had died. I can remember the day after he was buried, I took one of my nephews and went out to Evanston where I had grown up, just to walk around and look at the places where I had done things with my father.

Even after the children were grown and away from home, they looked to their parents for spiritual guidance at those crucial hours of decision. When a member of the family was considering a teaching ministry overseas, Dr. Culbertson wrote,

Your good letter was awaiting me on my arrival at Winona. You may be assured of our earnest prayers especially at this time. I wish I had the wisdom enough to give you the right answer, but you are right that each of us must face the Lord for His guidance for us. It is very easy to choose—on the basis of what is appealing to us, what seems advantageous—and then possibly be miserable for a protracted period while the Lord disciplines us. We are praying that no mistake may be made, whatever the place of service.

I think I can give you two words of advice, which may possibly be of help and which the Lord may be in. While I think the sense of call ought to be in anything you contemplate, it seems to me—in the light of all the background—that a special sense of call to a mission field is needed. To travel to————just to teach a college subject will not, in my judgment, suffice. Unless there is a sense of God's leading, of being there as a missionary service, I question thinking seriously of it. Has God put that burden on your heart? Has the Lord singled that country out, so that you can say nothing else matters and nothing else will do?

The second thing grows out of my own experience. I have found it most advisable to prayerfully come to a decision with Mother on all matters relating to the kind and place of our work. Such a decision is far more than just being able to say when the way gets hard, "We decided this together." It has the advantage of the mutual interplay of personalities aiding and strengthening one another. In matters of this kind, I'm sure it is not expecting too much to ask for unity of decision.

I appreciate your letter beyond any words of mine to convey. You are doing right in carefully and prayerfully tracking down all leads. Don't jump—until you are sure of His will.

When his oldest son, Robert, decided he had been called

to the ministry, he immediately wrote his father and received the following reply:

> First of all, I want you to know how pleased and happy I am that you have responded to God's call to go into the ministry. Neither your mother nor I wanted to push you in that or any other direction. We wanted you to be led of the Lord. We believe that you have been. However, I would be less than human if I did not rejoice to see a son of mine in the Christian ministry. Be assured of our daily prayers—not only as to the call extended by the good people of Coralville—but as [to] all your life and work.

> God has given you gifts. The advantage of your formal training will become more apparent as the days go on. The knowledge of the Word of God together with the quiet, rather informal manner of presentation, plus an evident love for people, are all gifts from our Lord. However, as important as these gifts are, never lose sight of the fact that the closeness in which you live in fellowship with the Lord will determine the true success of your ministry. I do not claim to have set the example here, but by God's grace —I have endeavored to pave the way.

> Never be afraid to play second fiddle for God. The Lord has His way of giving more opportunity, if we have been faithful in the ministry He grants us. Don't be afraid (I am glad that you are not) of the lowly, even the menial tasks. The way into the hearts of people is often very common.

After saying a few words of encouragement to Robert's wife, Dr. Culbertson concluded the letter with the kind of practical counsel that endeared him to all who ever sought direction from him.

> There are bound to be discouragements for you both. To keep sweet, to rest in the Lord, to look to God to do what only He can do, is the only answer. Remember, however,

for every burden God has His compensations. Souls you have been used to win, Christians who have been made strong by your preaching and by your living, friends along the way, enough for needs, and above all, the companionship of the Lord are more than enough to compensate for any trial.

One word more. Do make much of the Word of God. Preach the Word. Never preach your doubts. May you have a teaching ministry. Christians grow strong as they are fed the Word of God. May you be able to lead them into fields of service: Prayer, giving, testimony, evangelism. These things and many others are on my heart. For these matters your mother and I shall be praying.

Dr. Culbertson wrote that letter from his favorite vacation spot, the campgrounds at Mexico, Pennsylvania. Mrs. Culbertson's family had vacationed at Island Grove for years, and she grew up loving the rustic simplicity of "the humble little place." Less than a hundred people lived on the campgrounds during the summer, but on weekends and in the evenings during the camp meeting, many believers would drive in for the preaching services. Dr. Culbertson had visited Mexico a few times before their marriage; after that, they rented a cottage and then secured one of their own for their family.

Each August, the Island Grove Camp Meeting Association sponsored a ten-day camp meeting, and from the early 1930s, Dr. Culbertson was usually a featured speaker. Some years, he spoke every day of the meeting; but in later years, he concentrated on the Sunday services with an occasional prophetic message using his beautiful pictures of the Holy Land. (He was an excellent amateur photographer.) Many times, he led the Bible study sessions, while local pastors brought the main messages. He was a permanent honorary member of the general committee and was certainly a great spiritual encouragement to the entire ministry of the conference. In the 1958 conference folder, the committee paid him this tribute: "We are very thankful for the many years of his deep loyalty and faithfulness to our Camp Meeting. To know him is to love him; to have fellowship with him is to be strengthened in the Christian faith; and to hear him is to be challenged anew in a closer walk with God."

Dr. Culbertson often used the cottage at Mexico as the summer headquarters for his wider ministry, although he was careful to make that time meaningful as a family vacation. He called the place "the woods," and usually by August 1, he was ready to leave Chicago, put on his fishing togs, and enjoy the out-of-doors. His love for the campgrounds deepened from year to year: here he could be with the family and they could do things together, and here he was simply himself, another camper. To be sure, the other residents respected him highly. Most of them called him "Bishop" or, if they had known him through the years, as many of them had, just simply "Bill." No one was offended at his clothes, because this was the way everybody dressed. Mexico, for the bishop, was a very enriching "parenthesis" in the midst of a demanding life, and his friends there respected his privacy.

The facilities were quite rustic, including the lack of plumbing; but the four Culbertson children were willing to sacrifice their Evanston luxuries for the joys of spending four weeks with their parents, doing things that they could not do together the rest of the year. And when it came to doing things, fishing was on the top of the list. Dr. Culbertson was a good fisherman, especially with minnows; and he had his own private source of minnows that he carefully guarded. He and the boys would visit the stream and scare the minnows into the net, never taking more than they really could use. "At least in this respect," Paul observed, "Dad was ahead of the ecologists. He never believed in wasting what the Lord had provided." One year, Dr. Culbertson made the mistake of sharing his secret with another camper, and the man used up all the minnows and put an end to their private supply.

Even after the children left home, they often returned to Mexico for part of the family vacation; and this always meant several fishing trips for the three men. One day, Dr. Culbertson informed the boys that they were going to fish for "native trout," but first they had to get some nightcrawlers. At midnight, the three of them were stalking worms at an old canal bed, flashlights in hand. Early the next morning, they drove up a back road to a stream, and the bishop told the boys just where to fish. They were fortunate: they caught six trout, the biggest of which was eight inches. "My mother was the one who enjoyed trout the most," Paul observed. "He caught them primarily to please her."

Dr. Culbertson admired anyone who could work with his hands, although he did not consider himself gifted in that area. He did manage to keep up his house in Evanston and the simple cottage in Mexico, but he did not boast of any special abilities. One Mexico resident that he greatly admired was "Curley" Heeter, a master of many trades. One day Curley was making forms to pour a new cement porch and stairway, and for some reason, made a mistake in the work. He became so angry that he stormed into his cottage, got into his bathing suit, and went to the stream for a swim. Dr. Culbertson had been watching him, but he said nothing during the brief eruption. When Curley came back from his swim, he found that the bishop had carefully taken the forms apart for him so that now he could begin all over.

But the bishop never took a vacation from the ministry. Not only did he preach regularly, but he also tried to help people with their personal problems. One afternoon, he heard the news that the only daughter of a family in town had been killed in an auto accident; and the next day, he and Mrs. Culbertson visited the parents and sought to comfort them from the Word. He was not obligated to do this; it was something that was natural to his heart.

One day, a group of believers asked if he would baptize them in the old swimming hole. Since the Reformed Episcopal Church practices both sprinkling and immersion, Dr. Culbertson was happy to be of service. He donned some old clothes, walked into the swimming hole with the candidates, and immersed them.

His last visit to the campgrounds was in August 1971. He did not get a fishing license. The ache in his arm (which he diagnosed as arthritis) made the sport too painful; and he was content simply to rest and enjoy fellowship with his family and friends. He spoke at two of the area churches and at the camp meeting on Sunday afternoon and evening. He did a lot of walking; the solitude was refreshing and gave him opportunity for unhindered prayer and meditation. His weeks at Mexico that summer were a quiet preparation for the demands that he would meet back in Chicago. No one imagined it would be his last visit to a place and a group of people that he dearly loved.

There are two interesting postscripts to the camp meeting ministry. In 1972, Robert was to preach in his father's place; but the floods that destroyed so much property in Pennsylvania reached Mexico as well, and there was no conference that year. Perhaps it was just as well. The residents rebuilt their cabins and made a new beginning the next summer.

In 1973, Mrs. Culbertson and the family vacationed at the campgrounds again, missing the bishop very much but grateful for all that God had done. The leaders held a beautiful memorial service for Dr. Culbertson, at which they played the tape recording of his last sermon, preached September 5, 1971, at the AAJE conference at Winona Lake, Indiana. "I thought I was not going to be able to sit through it," Mrs. Culbertson confided, "but his voice was so real that you almost thought he was there. You found your-self glancing at the platform to see the preacher. I was grateful for the recording, because it gave a number of peo-ple opportunity to hear my husband preach who had never had the opportunity before. I know hearts were touched."

Of course, those who attended the memorial service knew that Mrs. Culbertson had been very much a part of the bish-op's ministry, even though she had kept herself in the back-ground. She told Ruth Bruckner in a *Moody Student* inter-view that, to be the president's wife, was "to be the person nobody knew." The wives of the Moody students knew her as a driving spiritual force behind the Women's Guild which met every Tuesday. At each meeting, she would en-courage them in their own spiritual lives and ministries, and would direct them in the building of homes that would glorify God. The wives of Christian workers have their own peculiar problems and needs, and Mrs. Culbertson knew how to meet them from the Word and from personal experi-ence.

"My prayer for you and for myself is that we end well."

"Culbertson Day" May 19, 1971

THIRTEEN

The Bishop Ends Well

When the Institute trustees met on September 22, 1970, the president reminded them that he would reach retirement age in two months and that it was imperative that they begin to seek God's leading concerning his successor. The men knew they would eventually have to make this decision, but nobody faced it gladly. During the twenty-two years of Dr. Culbertson's leadership, the school had experienced steady, stable growth, and was recognized around the world as a citadel of the evangelical faith. The bishop had guided its affairs during a difficult period of American church life, when fundamental Christianity was being fragmented into various opposing camps, any one of which would have been happy to influence the school. Without wavering one degree from the original doctrines, standards, or purposes of the school, Dr. Culbertson had maintained a positive, balanced ministry throughout that stormy era.

But many people were concerned about the future. He had been more than an administrator: he had been a shepherd, a spiritual father to the Institute family. Would it be possible to find another man who would guide the school into new areas of ministry without sacrificing the precious heritage that made the Moody Bible Institute so distinctive? Dr. Culbertson thought he knew such a man.

Chairman of the board of trustees, Elner A. Edman, had asked each of the members of the executive committee to hand in the names of possible candidates to be considered at their November 3 meeting. Wisely, Dr. Culbertson suggested that the committee first consider the qualifications for the position, then the names in the light of those qualifications, and then the procedure for bringing in the man of their choice. The committee agreed with these suggestions. It also voted unanimously to recommend to the board that Dr. Culbertson remain as president for another year to help in implementing the suggestions.

It was no ordinary man that they were seeking. He must love the Moody Bible Institute and be a firm believer in the Bible institute as a valid form of Christian training. He must be a preacher of the Word, able to speak to large audiences. He should be an administrator, able to keep the lines of ministry open and active. His convictions as to doctrine and Christian living must be those of the school; and he must not be identified with any particular wing of evangelical life. His ministry would have to be interdenominational no matter what his own beliefs might be. A number of names came before the committee, and all of them were discussed. The final decision would have to be made later.

Dr. Culbertson had a conviction in his heart that God had chosen his successor and that he was not very far away. On November 19, he had lunch at Chicago's Union League Club with Dr. George Sweeting, the senior pastor of Moody Memorial Church, a man who seemed to him to possess all the necessary qualifications for the presidency. Dr. Sweeting had come to Moody Church in August, 1966, when the ministry was at low ebb and the church had been without a pastor for over three years. Under his courageous, optimistic leadership, Moody Church took on a new look both physically and spiritually: attendance increased; the ministry expanded; and in every way, there was evidence of God's blessing. Dr. Sweeting had graduated from the Institute in 1945 and had served successfully as an evangelist and pastor. He had become a member of the Institute board of trustees in 1969 and certainly was committed to the ministry of the school.

"Although some of my fellow trustees had occasionally attempted to discover my personal feelings concerning the presidency," Dr. Sweeting recalls, "Dr. Culbertson himself never discussed the subject with me until November 19, 1970. We sat at a table in the spacious dining room of Chicago's Union League Club; and as we looked over the menu, Dr. Culbertson said in his deliberate way, 'It was at this very table, in this same dining room, many years ago, that Henry P. Crowell and Dr. Houghton urged me to come to the Institute. I've never regretted coming.'

"As he shared the burden of his heart, it was evident that the multiplied responsibilities of the Institute weighed heavily upon him. The thought of my coming to the Institute was not a total surprise to me; but as the reality of the situation was discussed, I was frankly overwhelmed, and I began, like Moses, to list all my inadequacies! Dr. Culbertson listened, and then reassuringly said, 'I believe you have the gifts and that under God you will lead the Institute to greater heights.' As we parted, we agreed to pray in earnest about the matter and seek God's will."

The executive committee met on December 1 to consider Dr. Sweeting as a possible successor to Dr. Culbertson; and on January 5, 1971, they voted unanimously to recommend him to the board of trustees, which was to meet two weeks later. The board met and accepted the recommendation, and at noon, Dr. Sweeting was asked to join the meeting. He told them quite frankly that he knew his name was under consideration, and that he was greatly honored and humbled by their decision; but he wanted more time to consider the matter.

On February 25, Dr. Sweeting sent this telegram to Dr.
Culbertson and to the chairman of the board, Elner A. Edman:

> AFTER MONTHS OF PRAYER AND DELIBERATE
> CONSIDERATION, I AM PREPARED TO ACCEPT
> THE HONOR AND RESPONSIBILITY OF BECOMING
> THE SIXTH PRESIDENT OF THE MOODY BIBLE IN-
> STITUTE. MY CONFIDENCE IS IN JESUS CHRIST
> ALONE WHO IS ALL-SUFFICIENT.

Dr. Culbertson immediately telephoned Dr. Sweeting and
expressed his great joy at the decision. "I feel like a load has
lifted," he said. When the board met again in April, the
official decision was made. Mr. James H. Barnes moved,
and Mr. E. Richard Tallmadge seconded, that the board
designate Dr. George Sweeting as president-elect, and that
Dr. Culbertson remain as president until July 31, 1971, and
then serve as chancellor beginning August 1.

Dr. Culbertson expressed his appreciation for the action
the board had taken, and assured them and the president-
elect that he would do everything possible to assist Dr.
Sweeting and promote the good of the school. "I am thankful to God for Dr. Sweeting, for the abilities God has given
him, for the evidence of God's hand upon him, and for the
Lord's leading in his call to the presidency. It is my desire
to stand behind the new president."

The president-elect expressed his gratitude to the board
for their confidence in calling him:

> I trust that by God's grace, I will merit the confidence you
> have demonstrated in me today. We are laborers together
> with God. My desire is, as much as I am able, to follow
> along in the same style and with the same program as Dr.
> Culbertson, with a few innovations. I want to encourage
> and support the faculty in every conceivable way, and
> maintain the same high standards and warm evangelistic

spirit in all classes. I am excited by the opportunities before us!

William Culbertson knew that the Institute would be in good hands. He remarked to Miss Hogan, "Dr. Sweeting's coming to Moody Church and to the Institute was certainly the Lord's timing." He told Mrs. Helen Wiggins, a cousin and an old friend of the family, "Now I'll have more time for Bible conference work." He was happy that the board had designated him chancellor and not president emeritus. "'President emeritus' sounds like they're putting me out to pasture!" he said. "And I don't intend to be put out to pasture!"

But there were those who had their doubts. One man wrote:

> I am sorry to bother you with a trifal [sic] matter, but I have a burden. At church the other night we were discussing the changes in the presidinticy [sic] of Moody Bible Institute. A couple of people who said that they had thought they would go to Moody changed their minds. The reason for the uproar is that we are afraid that when you leave the president's chair at Moody, that Moody will start to slide downhill. In other words, sir, we are afraid that Moody will start to compromise her position and will start going with the liberal churches. . . . We know that Moody's slide will not happen in one year, but will take five or ten years to fully happen. I love Moody and appreciate what it has done for me.

The bishop's reply should have calmed the brother's fears.

> I am sure, my dear brother, if you knew how careful our Board of Trustees was in the selection of a new president and the items that concerned them—having to do with doctrine and standards of Christian living—your concern for the future of the Institute would be much less. I thank

God for these men of God and I believe they have had
the leading of the Lord. I, of course, joined with them in
the action taken.

Let me express to you how much we appreciate your concern and how much we count upon your prayers. I believe that, if the Lord tarries, there are glorious days ahead
at Moody Bible Institute.

Most of the mail that came in after the announcement
was encouraging, and Dr. Culbertson appreciated each letter. Dr. Rene Pache wrote from the Emmaus Institute in
Switzerland:

Through Miss Helen Needham, I hear that you have been
appointed as Chancellor of the Institute and I have even
seen the thrilling paper with all the photos, etc.

May I send you my warmest congratulations and express
my admiration for the wonderful work you have done,
not only for the Institute but also for the Lord's work
throughout the world. How glorious will the day of the
great harvest be, when all the young people trained by
you will bring in their sheaves before the Lord. May He
daily renew your strength and bless your further ministry
for many years to come.

He also heard from the President of the United States,
Richard M. Nixon:

It has come to my attention that you have recently completed two decades as President of Moody Bible Institute
and have accepted the post of Chancellor of this distinguished organization.

Your selfless and successful efforts to spread the word
and work of God on earth have earned you the admiration
of all who recognize the value of religion in our lives and
in the life of our nation.

My congratulations to you for all the good you have achieved and my best wishes for the fullest measure of satisfaction in the years ahead as you further enhance your splendid reputation in the course of your new duties.

His friend, Dr. John W. Bradbury, editor and preacher, with whom he had shared prophetic conferences, sent his greetings also.

We have known one another over many years, therefore I feel free to express to you the warm affection and admiration I have always felt for you. The standard you have exalted for the glory of our blessed Redeemer has never trembled or wilted but remains a memorable banner of confidence, inspiration and hope.

The years take their toll. Our ministry improves. We get more done by doing less. It is also better. My own experience demonstrates this. You are now at the time when the fruit is ripe and ready. You do not need any courses in Christian evidences, you have had it. The slightest pressure on the grape will bring forth the nectar of life. The Lord is at hand, always true, but now very real. God will continue to bless you.

But it was not only the great and famous who wrote him; he also heard from his beloved "sons and daughters" in the Institute student body. One girl wrote:

Congratulations as you take your new position as Chancellor of the Institute! I want to take this opportunity to thank you for your past ministry as President. You will never know the impact your Monday morning chapels had on me. God greatly used you there, not only in my life, but in the lives of many of my fellow-students.

Now, as our first Chancellor, it will be exciting to watch God work through you in this new ministry. As you know, God has used you to influence a great many people, and the great wisdom He has given you is evident. If I were to decide my impression of you, it would be more than anything else that you have walked with God. My prayer is that He will continue to use you and bless you as He has so faithfully done in the past.

Because I am a senior, I remember many times when you called us your sons and daughters. May I take this opportunity to say, my love and prayers go with you, Dad.

But the students did more than write letters: they secretly planned a "Culbertson Day" celebration for May 19. Student Council leaders Jack Vanaman, Gary Gulbranson, Greg Waybright, assisted by radio producer Ken Apple, and *Moody Student* editor Mike Farrell, engineered the feat with the cooperation of Mrs. Culbertson and Miss Hogan. The May 21 *Moody Memo* called the program "a masterpiece of organization. It moved nostalgically through a pictorial memory lane from year one in the Culbertson household to the present era, including an outstanding rendition of 'The Sands of Time Are Sinking' (one of Dr. Culbertson's favorite hymns) by the combined MBI choirs, and brought together an impressive group of evangelical dignitaries who gave thrilling tribute to MBI's fifth president."

Among the dignitaries were J. Palmer Muntz, William Kuhnle, Elner Edman, Kenneth McQuere, Dr. Alfred Martin, and Dr. John Walvoord (with whom he had worked on the *New Scofield Reference Bible*). President-elect Sweeting and Dr. Irwin Moon, director of the Moody Institute of Science, were unable to attend and sent greetings. A special edition of the *Moody Student* featured priceless photos of Dr. Culbertson and members of the family. The issue was released earlier than expected that day, and Miss Hogan had to frantically phone around Crowell Hall to make sure the president did not see a copy. The climax of the hour-long program was the releasing of a twenty-seven-foot banner that soared to the ceiling of Torrey-Gray Auditorium and announced: "We love you, Dr. Culbertson!"

A telegram from Dr. Billy Graham said:

> While the student bodies of many educational institutions jeer their president, I am thrilled to learn of one great institution that is *cheering* its president. No man in our generation has stood so faithfully for the gospel as has Dr. Culbertson. He has led Moody Bible Institute during one of the most turbulent periods of history.

The president's response to the occasion was typical: "God bless you! I am overwhelmed. My emotions have run the gamut. Thank you for the tributes. My one desire for you is that God will help you to end well as you walk humbly before Him." Later, in his office, he confessed: "It was a very wonderful occasion—so well planned and executed. While I question I deserved it, nevertheless, it is appreciated. My hearty thanks to all." To student leader Greg Waybright, who had emceed the program, he wrote:

> This is just a note to try to express my deep appreciation for the Recognition Day on Wednesday of last week. I do not know of any occasion that has been carried off more to perfection and so movingly. I think it is wonderful that with so many people being involved no one even whispered a suggestion to me, so that the surprise you had in mind was fully accomplished.

> Your love means more to me than I can express. Please share with the student council and the student body my own love and gratitude for you all. And do convey my special thanks and commendation to those who worked so hard to put on a program that, in my judgment, could not have been improved upon. Mrs. Culbertson and indeed the whole family thank you from their hearts.

> Thank you too for the additional item that came to the

attention of Faculty last Monday—the report in the Congressional Record of May 19. You surely left no stone unturned The recognition, though utterly beyond anything I deserve, is appreciated most deeply.

To *Moody Student Editor* Mike Farrell, he wrote:

Let me thank you for all that you and your colleagues on the *Moody Student* did in connection with the Recognition Day. I understand you were a prime mover and I do want you to know that I appreciate all that you did. The issue of the *Moody Student* is far more devoted to me than I ever deserve, but I know what is in your heart and I am grateful for your love and loyalty.

It was general knowledge that Dr. Culbertson avoided any kind of public recognition. In 1950, he had led the Institute family in the dedication of Houghton Hall, named after his honored predecessor; but when the trustees decided to name the new men's dormitory Culbertson Hall, he had tried to dissuade them but was unsuccessful. When the announcement was made at a special employee chapel session at the opening of school in 1968, the audience spontaneously broke into loud applause, much to the embarrassment of their president. Yet he helped to dedicate the finished building on September 22, 1970, reminding the gathered friends, "This building and this campus are evidence that there is a living God!" He knew that the modern, twenty-two-story building would house hundreds of young men who would train for Christian service, and, after all, that was why he came to the Institute in the first place. Perhaps that day, he remembered the words of J. D. Adams, "Young man, how would you like to multiply your life a thousand times?"

The school year ended on a note of triumph. God was changing His workmen, but His work was going on. Little did anyone realize that, for their beloved chancellor, the end was very near.

*   *   *

Dr. and Mrs. Culbertson spent much of the summer of 1971 away from Chicago. They ministered in Great Britain and then took their usual family holiday at Mexico, Pennsylvania. Miss Hogan seemed to detect a different attitude in her boss when he returned from British Keswick, "as though he didn't seem interested anymore—which was very unlike him." When he left for the Island Grove Camp meeting, he told her, "I'll not lock my desk. You transfer the stuff for me, please." And she did, collecting the little slips of paper with outlines on them, plus the clippings he had saved for future use.

It was clear to those who knew him well that the bishop was not himself, that he was fighting a physical battle. Eight years before, while attending the October meeting of the Accrediting Association, he had developed a problem; and the doctor, on examining him, had immediately scheduled him for surgery at Chicago's Swedish Covenant Hospital. It turned out to be a malignancy in the colon; but the surgery had been a success, and Dr. Culbertson had returned to the office by December. He attended the retirement dinner for his good friend Coleman Crowell, and had even made it to the employees' annual Christmas party. It took a year for him to get back to his regular schedule, but tests every six months had revealed that his condition was excellent.

Then in May 1970, one of the tests had revealed a spot on the lung, even though Dr. Culbertson was complaining of no special problems. Knowing the medical history, the surgeon ordered an operation; and while commencement exercises were in rehearsal at Torrey-Gray Auditorium, the president was under the scapel. Once again, the Lord was gracious to answer prayer, and he recovered. He had to cancel his summer schedule, including the annual Moody Alumni Conference at Winona Lake, Indiana. He was able to visit the conference one day, since Winona Lake is only a three-hour drive from Chicago. Alumni executive secretary, Ken McQuere, asked him to lead in prayer.

"I cannot preach to you," he said, as he stepped to the microphone, "but I can pray for you. And this is only right, because so many of you have been praying for me. I can only say that the Lord is answering prayer, and we all have much to thank Him for. Now, let us pray." And he lifted the hushed congregation to the Throne.

Now, on the threshold of a new ministry, it seemed that the old problem had reappeared. When he returned from the family holiday, he had a nagging pain in the back. At the September 28 trustees meeting, he told Mr. Harry Dykstra, "I feel pretty good—except for the pain in my back." That evening, he presided at the inauguration of the new president. "But," said Miss Hogan, "I don't know how he got through it!" His son Robert, pastor of the Calvary Bible Church, Boulder, Colorado, led in the prayer of commitment. The bishop, as always, made the service a high and holy one, but it was easy to see that he was fighting a battle. Even the pictures that appeared in the Chicago newspapers the next day indicate he was in pain.

"The next day," recalls Miss Hogan, "Dr. Culbertson almost staggered into the office. Several times, his hand slipped when he tried to do something, and he couldn't hold up his right arm. He was having difficulty walking. On October 5, he recorded a tape for WMBI, finishing a series on the thrones of the Bible; but his voice broke several times and seemed to lack the usual vibrancy and power. We knew something was wrong."

On October 6, he entered Swedish Covenant hospital for

the third time in less than ten years. Tests indicated that the lung cancer had returned, and he was immediately given treatments. His condition varied from day to day, but he was able to have visitors, and his general progress indicated that he might be released by his birthday, November 18. Dr. Sweeting stopped often and carried his greetings to his "sons and daughters" at the campus. On November 9, Dr. Culbertson wrote the students:

> Your prayers, your loving concern, and your messages of encouragement have been a great blessing to me during these past weeks. I am thankful to the Lord that a recent x-ray indicates definite improvement, and I am looking forward to continued recovery, in His will, in the days ahead. "O give thanks unto the Lord, for He is good; for His mercy endureth forever." God bless you all.

When the florist delivered a huge crystal planter from "Your sons and daughters," the bishop was deeply stirred and openly wept. "Can you imagine them doing this for me?" he told a visitor. "I really don't deserve their love, but they love me just the same, I guess!"

In his own quiet, loving way, Dr. Culbertson witnessed to the different roommates that came and went during his six weeks in the hospital. His last roommate was a Chicago policeman who showed a keen interest in the gospel because of Dr. Culbertson's witness. Those who went in and out of the room knew that no ordinary patient was in that bed. Even in pain and weakness, Dr. Culbertson quietly radiated the love of Christ.

So definite was his improvement that everyone expected him to be home by the middle of November. "My wife is promising me baked Alaska for my birthday," he commented to a visiting pastor, "and I intend to eat it *at home!*" His visitors remarked how much better he looked, and he made it clear that he was feeling better. He had received many encouraging letters from friends across the nation whose assurances of prayer help and love inspired him greatly. Dr. Wilbur Smith wrote:

> In the dual areas of illness and friendship nothing could grieve me as much as to know you are back again in the hospital. The older I grow the greater seems (to me) this mystery of pain, in the lives of dedicated servants of the Lord. Two results are, of course, revealed—one is the truthfulness of St. James' remark that life is but a vapor. The other is that it drives us to the throne of grace, especially on the part of loved ones and closest friends. . . . Every life you have touched has been for blessing. May our gracious Lord continue to be near you. You mean so much to me personally.

Dr. and Mrs. Stephen Olford telegraphed:

> JUST HEARD YOU ARE IN THE HOSPITAL AGAIN AND WANT TO ASSURE YOU OF OUR THOUGHTS, LOVE AND PRAYERS. MAY DEUTERONOMY 33:27 BE VERY PRECIOUS TO YOU. REMEMBERING YOUR DEAR WIFE AFFECTIONATELY.

And his dear friend, and MBI trustee, Jacob Stam, wrote:

> Bob Constable has been kind to let me know of your troubles and that you are back in the hospital. With grateful memories my mind goes back to when we first met at the Stearns Fund Board meeting; to our long correspondence about joining the Moody Board; to our trip to Connecticut to meet those rugged, conservative Yankee supporters; to years of service together on the Moody Board, and lately the months of correspondence, mostly from you, keeping me up to date. I thank God upon every remembrance. And now for this additional experience of physical suffering and hospitalization, I trust that more than ever you will experience the grace that IS sufficient; that

more than ever you will have the comfort of the Scriptures. Be assured of our prayers for you. Best wishes to Mrs. Culbertson.

The delegates of Accrediting Association of Bible Colleges, at their twenty-fifth annual meeting, sent him the following resolution:

> Inasmuch as Dr. William Culbertson has served the Accrediting Association of Bible Colleges as one of its founders, as a member of the Executive Committee and several Commissions, and as President, and inasmuch as his personal life of deep devotion to Jesus Christ has been an example to all of us, and inasmuch as we love him as a friend and brother, be it resolved that we express our love, extend our sympathy and assure him of our prayers in this his time of sickness and trial, and as a token send a plant to him.

Everyone who visited him on November 16 commented about how good he looked. His wife and May Hogan stopped that evening, but Miss Hogan had to leave early because of a ladies' meeting at her home. Jovially, Dr. Culbertson called after her, "Greet the ladies for me!" That statement was part of a family joke that stemmed from an incident that week. Two elderly ladies from one of the Chicago churches had visited him in the hospital, and though they were total strangers to him, he received them with his usual graciousness. Imagine his surprise when, as they were leaving, one of the ladies came over to his bed and kissed him on the cheek! "She kissed me right there!" he told a visiting friend, pointing to the place. "I should recover after that!"

But recovery was not a part of God's plan, even though it was the heart's desire of all who knew and loved him. At 11:30 that night, November 16, God called him home. His final words were, "God—God—yes!" He died as he had lived, in the will of God.

*   *   *

Dr. Culbertson's body lay in state in Torrey-Gray Auditorium where he had so often ministered to his "sons and daughters" at the Monday morning chapel services, and where each year he had addressed the great Founder's Week crowds. Mr. Willis Mayfield, vice-president of the development branch, arranged for an honor guard. Various Institute students and employees were selected to take turns standing at the head and the foot of the coffin. It was November 18, his sixty-sixth birthday. All classes were cancelled for the one o'clock memorial service. It was a dignified, Christ-exalting service, led by Dr. George Sweeting, whose opening words set the keynote: "We will have a service of triumphant praise as we worship the Lord together!" He read John 14:1-6 and 1 Thessalonians 4:13-18. WMBI radio personality Bill Pearce sang Dr. Culbertson's favorite hymn, "King Most Wonderful," as well as another much-loved song, "The Sands of Time Are Sinking." The Men's Glee Club sang "Sun of My Soul" and "All Hail the Power." Dr. Culbertson's long-time friend, and a successor at Grace Church in Collingdale, Dr. Edwin Bustard, gave a stirring "Tribute to A Friend," closing with: "The greatest tribute we can give him is to follow in the steps of his matchless Saviour."

President Sweeting's message centered on the Christian view of death, and it sounded the note of confidence and the expectation of glory. "Death to the Christian is a loosing— an anchors aweigh—freedom at last to enter glory!" One of the most moving parts of the service was the reciting of Psalm Twenty-Three by the entire congregation. Mr. Constable appropriately concluded the service by quoting the benediction Dr. Culbertson had voiced so often, a poem written by John Newton:

> May the grace of Christ our Saviour,
> And the Father's boundless love,
> With the Holy Spirit's favor,
> Rest upon us from above.
>
> Thus may we abide in union
> With each other and the Lord,
> And possess, in sweet communion,
> Joys which earth cannot afford. Amen.

There were scores of cars in the procession that made its way to Memory Gardens, in nearby Arlington Heights, where Dr. Culbertson's body was laid to rest. His lifelong prayer had been answered: he had ended well.

*"I have stood in the place of tempta-
tion. I have stood at the place where
I might have wavered and gone the
other way. And if I hadn't, it's no
credit to me; it's only credit to the Son
of God, and to those who prayed and
God answered their prayers."*

Founder's Week, 1956

FOURTEEN

In Reflection

"Very few people really knew my father," Paul Culbertson once remarked to me. "In many ways my dad was a
very private person. There were not too many people with
whom he really felt comfortable and let his hair down. I
should add, when I say this, the fact that when he did let
his hair down, there was nothing contradictory about that
as to what he said in public. What he actually *was* and
what he *said* were the same thing."

William Culbertson was not a complex person, nor was he
a man who played different roles as the situation demanded. He was one of the most consistent of men, and it was his
consistent simplicity that marked him as a man of depth
and practical godliness. "The moment you become verbose,
the moment you become garrulous," he told the 1956
Founder's Week audience, "it's good evidence that it's pretty
much on the surface." William Culbertson was not a shal-
low man, and therefore he was not a talkative man. It was
this quiet, serious attitude of life that disarmed the religious

trifler who wanted to impress him; but this same devotion attracted believers who understood that the Christian life was a battleground, not a playground.

Certainly he was the product of a serious Christian home. As an only child, he had time to ponder, to discover the values of solitude, and to make early in life the kind of choices that would direct him for years to come. His personal character and characteristics, as well as the opportunities he had as a youth to hear great men of God, all combined to influence him toward Christian dedication and ministry. We need not fight again the ancient battle between "nature" and "nurture," because both play an important part in the shaping of a man. But we do need to recognize the fact that, in the providence of God, William Culbertson was gifted of God for the work of the ministry, and was privileged to have parents, pastors, and friends, who encouraged him in the development of these gifts.

The emphasis of his life was practical godliness, and he sought to experience for himself what he expounded to others. The "Faculty Tribute" to Dr. Culbertson, issued after his death, described him as a "man who disciplined himself physically, mentally, and spiritually," a man who "always seemed to know what to do, when to do it, and how to get it done." He had a "delicate balance between the practical and the spiritual." To Dr. Culbertson, the "victorious Christian life" was not a single crisis that solved every problem. There was no place in his thinking for "instant Christianity." In a 1957 Keswick message, he said, "It is my profound conviction that no Christian will know true holy living by indolence, by carelessness, by trying to find some shortcut to sanctification." He would have agreed with George Morrison, who said, "The victorious Christian life is a series of new beginnings."

Nor was he exempt from the human problems and sufferings of life. His theology was refined in the furnace, not in the ivory tower. "Many of God's choicest secrets and blessings are only discovered when we are shut in and shut up to Him," he wrote in a *Moody Monthly* editorial. "The valley can become the place of vision." In his 1970 Founder's Week message, he opened his heart to his listeners when he said:

> I have been a pastor, and I have been in administrative posts of Moody Bible Institute for many, many years. Don't you think, my dear friends, that those years have all passed in tranquility. Don't you think that there have not been times when the devil has gotten his licks in and he in great power has pushed me down into the dust of defeat, for his attacks have been severe—not only against me personally, but against the work of God; and my heart has been broken, and I have shed tears.

No doubt, he was referring in part to those instances of disagreement and misunderstanding, and perhaps even of discipline, that are part of the history of every ministry, no matter how spiritual it may be. Whenever Dr. Culbertson was confronted with facts about a fellow worker, he investigated them carefully; and if the person was guilty, action was quick and final. But Dr. Culbertson always felt the hurt within his own heart.

After reading hundreds of his letters, I am impressed with the gentle spirit he exercised when replying to people whose attitudes were not only hostile, but often abusive. No doubt, these letters cut him deeply when he first read them, but I can see him, like Hezekiah of old, spreading them before the Lord, praying over them, and then replying in the spirit of love and kindness. A man in his position was vulnerable to attacks from all sides: to some, he was too liberal; to others, he was too fundamental! I recall chatting with him one day after a popular news magazine had run an article on the Institute, in which they accused the school of being too conservative. That same week, a local pastor had attacked the school for being too liberal. Dr. Culbertson smiled and quietly said to me, "Well, this week, you can take your choice!"

Dr. Culbertson was fundamental in his convictions, but he was not militant in his methods. He sought to practice Bible separation as the Spirit of God led him, but he did not seek to force others to follow his convictions. He was definite, but not dogmatic. You knew where he stood, but he did not expect you to stand with him unless you held the same convictions. Even his enemies (and he had a few) had to admit that he was a godly man whose life was a blessing to others. He often warned against "the substitution of vehemency in defense of the faith for vitality in living the faith."

There were those who felt he was weak in the matter of administration, and yet the record does not bear this out. During his twenty-nine years at the Institute, the physical campus was dramatically changed, the curriculum improved, and the spiritual life strengthened. It had always been a great school, but under his leadership, it became even greater. In 1949, the missionary technical course was inaugurated. The new girls' dormitory, Houghton Hall, was dedicated in 1951, and the Torrey-Gray Auditorium was completed and dedicated in 1955. In 1958, WCRF in Cleveland, Ohio, began its radio ministry; and in 1960, WDLM in East Moline, Illinois, and WMBI-FM in Chicago, began broadcasting. Fitzwater Hall was dedicated in 1962 to provide additional classroom space as well as offices for the faculty. The degree program, announced in 1965, was a monumental step forward in Christian higher education. Of course, the erection of Culbertson Hall was a tremendous accomplishment, opening the doors to more men desiring training at the Institute. And when you consider that Dr. Culbertson was also writing, sharing in a wider conference ministry, working with the Moody Institute of Science, helping edit the *New Scofield Reference Bible*, giving guidance to the Accrediting Association of Bible Colleges, and sharing in the ministry of Jewish evangelism, you come to the conclusion that he did know how to manage his time and get things done! Perhaps the thing that irritated his critics was his deliberation in making decisions, waiting until the facts were in and the Lord had given direction. This is not always a popular approach with some people.

As an administrator, Dr. Culbertson believed in working through channels. His strong right arm was executive vice-president and general manager, Robert L. Constable, a man whose dedicated service to God and the Institute gave great strength and guidance during Dr. Culbertson's administration. The two men were one at heart, not only in the spiritual essentials of the ministry, but in the goals and principles for the work of the school. Dr. Culbertson respected his associates in the work, and he was careful to "keep the lines clear and busy."

God gave him the wisdom and grace to guide the Moody Bible Institute during one of the most turbulent periods of American church history. He kept the school true to the faith, and he sought to make its ministry even more effective in contemporary life. Dr. George Sweeting described him perfectly in his tribute:

> Dr. Culbertson was a steadfast and courageous soul. Though gracious and gentle, he was rock-like in his convictions. He surely was not a reed blown about by every new breeze. He loved the Word of God and passionately and wholeheartedly embraced the fundamentals of the faith.

In an era when it was popular to identify with one movement or another, he ministered to the whole church and sought to maintain the distinctive interdenominational character of the school. Dr. Robert A. Cook, president of The King's College and a noted Moody alumnus, expressed it this way in a letter to Dr. Culbertson:

> In the larger sense, however, you belong to all of God's people. Not only in your leadership of the Institute, but also in your own monumental ministry, you have become to thousands a symbol of biblical stability and spiritual dynamics—a man who clearly proclaims God's truth in a day of dangerously fuzzy concepts and sagging morals.

He had a wonderful sense of humor that never became a weapon to hurt others or a device to attract attention to himself. He never joked about spiritual things, and he had no time for what Phillips Brooks called "the clerical jester." Jack Minter, chief security officer at the Institute, likes to tell about the morning he stopped the bishop on campus and asked, "Dr. Culbertson, do you know why the elephant painted his toenails red?" The bishop had to confess that he did not know. "So he could hide in the strawberry patch!" Minter said, and both of the men laughed.

The next morning, Dr. Culbertson came through the arch into Crowell Hall later than usual, and Minter thought he would tease him just a bit.

"You're late, Dr. Culbertson!" he said. "Where have you been?"

"Oh, out in the strawberry patch looking for elephants," was the quiet reply, and both men laughed even harder than they had the day before.

May Hogan recalls another elephant incident. Someone had given Dr. Culbertson a set of carved elephants to put on his desk. As he was leaving the office that afternoon, he heard Miss Hogan ask, "Aren't you going to take your elephants home with you?" Without pausing or glancing back at the animals, Dr. Culbertson replied, "Let them walk home by themselves." And out he went.

Of course, there were comical things that happened at home. The oldest children remember when little Ruth wanted a kitten. Dr. Culbertson was fond of cats, but at that particular time in the family's history, the presence of a cat was definitely inexpedient. Finally, Mrs. Culbertson told Ruth to pray about the problem, never dreaming that the little girl would do her best to answer her own prayers. Sure enough, the next day "God answered prayer," and Ruth came home with a kitten she had found. Her father was quite upset, but what could he do? Oddly enough, the cat liked only one member of the family—the bishop. "That cat was the most independent, ill-mannered beast that you could have found," Paul recalls. "When I would come home from college on visits, it would be Dad who was holding the cat! Somehow it seemed like just deserts."

Dr. Culbertson was a collector of clippings, and his desk drawers were filled with them. He also had a collection of filing cards with choice quotations and thoughts written on them in his distinctive script—which at times even he could not read! Here are some random samples:

> The test of character is how much opposition you can withstand and overcome.

> The greatest ability is dependability.

> If you don't have brains, borrow them!

> Hearts harden most quickly when men are trusting in their place of special privilege, without fellowship with the God Who gives it (Newell on *Romans*).

> Four words describe Christianity: Admit, Submit, Commit, Transmit (Bishop Wilberforce).

He kept a long quotation on humility from Andrew Murray,

written in his own hand, as well as his own handwritten copy of McCheyne's poem "Jehovah-Tsidkenu." He was a great admirer of J. Stuart Holden, and often quoted his statement: "Christ does not want *a place* in our lives, or *prominence* in our lives, but *preeminence*."

He would not be drawn into useless controversies and discussions. "Don't argue about so many things that you obscure the main thing," he often counselled his younger brethren in the ministry. While ministering at the Sandy Cove, Maryland, Bible Conference one summer, he found himself seated at the table with several pastors who were discussing the use of wine at the Lord's Supper. One man was vehemently opposing the use of it, and went so far as to say, "If I were ever at a communion service where wine was used, *I would spit it out!*" Since nobody at the table immediately responded to his statement, he turned and asked Dr. Culbertson, "And what would *you* do?"

"I had wine only once at a communion service," he quietly replied. "It was a common cup, so I couldn't spit it out."

He was a man who believed in, and depended on, the power of prayer. Dr. R. A. Torrey's classic book *The Power of Prayer* meant much to him, and he read it often. "Oh, how God has excoriated this cold heart of mine about my prayerlessness!" he confessed in a sermon. "For, you see, prayer doesn't come easily and naturally, and it isn't something we like to do in our fleshly natures." He told the 1957 Keswick Convention, "A dear saint of God—how she prayed for this poor preacher; and if in any measure there has been the blessing of God in my life, a great part of it is due to her."

That "dear saint of God" was his mother-in-law, Mrs. W. R. Gantz. After she passed away, Dr. Culbertson often said that he "missed something" in his life because she was no longer there to pray for him.

Perhaps the thing that most impresses us as we review his life is his courage to do the will of God in spite of circumstances or personal feelings. When he came to the Moody Bible Institute, he came as an educator and teacher. The death of Will H. Houghton dramatically changed his plans, and thrust him into the president's office. In some respects, he felt dwarfed by Dr. Houghton; and more than once, he reminded the trustees that they could secure another president if they felt he was not doing the job! It was a repetition of his decision to go to Germantown and tackle the problems of a divided church; or his decision to accept a bishopric because it would unite and strengthen the denomination, even though it meant sacrifice and more work for himself. "The subtle temptation is always to take it easy," he said to his 1958 Founder's Week address, "and somehow our friends help us out." An anonymous poem found in his desk expresses his feelings about the matter:

> No time for trifling in this life of mine;
>   Not this the path the blessed Master trod.
> But strenuous toil, each hour and power employed
>   Always and all for God.
>
> Time swiftly flies, eternity is near,
>   And soon my dust may lie beneath the sod.
> How dare I waste my life or cease to be
>   Always and all for God?
>
> I catch the meaning of this solemn age,
>   With life's vast issues all my soul is awed.
> Life was not given for trifling, it must be
>   Always and all for God.
>
> I hear the footfalls of God's mighty hosts
>   Whom God is sending all the earth abroad;
> Like them let me be busy for His cause
>   Always and all for God.

In a telegram read at the memorial service, Dr. Wilbur M. Smith said: "He was the most consecrated leader of any Christian school in America. Goodness and truth marked all that he did and said." Billy Graham called him "one of the most godly men I have ever known." Dr. Culbertson would have blushed at hearing such words and, with Paul, would have protested that he was chief of sinners.

Among the clippings Miss Hogan found in his desk was a poem that apparently was very meaningful to Dr. Culbertson. As we look back, we can understand why.

> Lord, when Thou seest that my work is done,
> Let me not linger on with failing powers,
> Adown the weary hours:
> A workless worker in a world of work;
> But with a word, just bid me home,
> And I will come right gladly,
> Yes, right gladly will I come!

"God—God—yes!"

He often wrote "Isaiah 32:17" beneath his signature. It is a verse we can write over his life:

> And the work of righteousness shall be peace; and the effect of righteousness quietness and assurance for ever.

This last message by Dr. Culbertson was preached at Winona Lake, Indiana, September 5, 1971.

FIFTEEN

What Will the Lord Say to Us All When He Returns?

by William Culbertson

We have been thinking together about the coming of the Lord for His own, when "the Lord himself shall descend from heaven, with a shout, with the voice of the archangel, and with the trump of God: and the dead in Christ shall rise first; then we that are alive, that are left, shall together with them be caught up in the clouds, to meet the Lord in the air: and so shall we ever be with the Lord." I remember a number of years ago in my study thinking about the coming of the Lord, contemplating what it will be to look on His lovely face, and the thought came to me: *I wonder what He will say to us all.* And I began to thumb through my Bible to see if there was any suggestion that might be applicable to the question I was raising. Ultimately, I turned to the book of the Song of Solomon, and I found what I believe may well be what the Lord will say to us all when He returns.

Now please, I understand that the Song of Solomon is a book all by itself, and I agree that it is the story of an actual courtship which has been preserved for us because of its spiritual application; and it tells us something of the love of

166

the Lord and what our love for the Lord ought to be. And the narrative with all of its Orientalisms, vivid and startling to the Occidental, ought to be read with the realization that it presents not simply a courtship but another love which is higher, holier, and fuller than all. Let me also acknowledge that what I read and the application I will make of it is not its primary thrust. I know something of the movement of the book. But I want to take a section of chapter 2 and think about it as suggestive of what the Lord Jesus may say to you and me when He comes again. I recognize that the primary thrust has its relationship to the lover and the one loved in the book. I recognize also that there are applications of it which impinge upon our relationship to the Lord. But let me take it from its context and let me apply it specifically to the Lord at His coming for His own.

Verse 8, chapter 2 of the book of Song of Solomon: the bride is speaking. She says, "The voice of my beloved! behold, he cometh." Now if I need to prove anything, I think the application, even though it's secondary, that I am making, is fully substantiated by the words I have just read. "Behold, he cometh, Leaping upon the mountains, Skipping upon the hills. My beloved is like a roe or a young hart: Behold, he standeth behind our wall; He looketh in at the windows; He glanceth through the lattice. My beloved spake, and said unto me"—that's what I'm after. "My beloved spake, and said unto me," reports the bride, "Rise up, my love, my fair one, and come away. For, lo, the winter is past; The rain is over and gone; The flowers appear on the earth; The time of the singing of birds is come, And the voice of the turtle-dove is heard in our land; The fig tree ripeneth her green figs, And the vines are in blossom; They give forth their fragrance. Arise, my love, my fair one, and come away. O my dove, that art in the clefts of the rock, In the covert of the steep place, Let me see thy countenance . . . thy countenance is comely."

There are just three things I would like to bring to your attention in connection with this message. First of all, it seems to me that the word the Lord speaks to the bride is an expression of an invitation. In the second place, it is the expression of the cessation of trial. And third, it is the expression of deepest love and holiest ardor.

It is the expression of an invitation. You notice it in verse 10: "Rise up, my love, my fair one, and come away." You see it again in verse 13, the end of the verse: "Arise, my love, my fair one, and come away." It seems to me this is very suitable language for our Lord as He comes. We are told in 1 Thessalonians 4:16 that He will shout. What will he shout? Well, perhaps it's this: "Rise up, my love, my fair one, and come away." He will speak to us. You'll remember that the Lord is the Lord Himself who descends from heaven, and He speaks, "Rise up, my fair one, my beloved, and come away." I think we have a suggestion of this also in the book of Revelation in chapter 4 where we begin the section of the epistle which has to do with the coming days. John says, "After these things I saw, and behold, a door opened in heaven, and the first voice that I heard, a voice as of a trumpet speaking with me, one saying, Come up hither." And that experience of John has been taken by many of us as exemplary of what will happen when the Lord comes for us. He will say "Come up hither," or in the language of the Song of Solomon, "Rise up, my love, my fair one, and come away." So it is the sound of His voice for which we wait.

And did you notice in the Song of Solomon two epithets are used, two appellations are used: "my love, my fair one." In thinking about that, I remembered how that on occasion the Lord would repeat a name, not just content to use one expression, but in repetition to speak a name twice. For example, in the twenty-second chapter of Genesis, the story of Abraham and Isaac. You'll recall that they were living in

Beersheba, and God's word came to Abraham. And so he left Beersheba and made his way northward to the land of Moriah, and he took with him Isaac his son and his servants. He took with him the wood for the fire, and made his way northward to the vicinity of Jerusalem, perhaps to the very place where the temple later stood. And as he made his way there, you will recall Isaac plaintively asked the question: "I see the wood, I see the fire; but where is the lamb?" And you will recall how that when they got to Moriah, Abraham built an altar and laid the wood in order, and then was stayed in what he was about to do in giving Isaac as a sacrifice.

Let me read it for you, "And they came to the place which God had told him of; and Abraham built the altar there, and laid the wood in order, and bound Isaac his son, and laid him on the altar, upon the wood. And Abraham stretched forth his hand, and took the knife to slay his son. And the angel of Jehovah called unto him out of heaven, and said, Abraham, Abraham: and he said, Here am I. And he said, Lay not thy hand upon the lad, neither do thou anything unto him; for now I know that thou fearest God, seeing thou hast not withheld thy son, thine only son, from me." The angel of the Lord, a preincarnate manifestation of the second Person of the holy Trinity, stayed the hand of Abraham, but spoke his name: "Abraham, Abraham." I've often tried to think of how that name was spoken. I think there must have been infinite tenderness in it and very wonderful recognition of the faith of Abraham. God spoke his name twice. And so when He comes for His own He'll say: "My love, my fair one."

Or do you recall how that in the desert of Sinai, at the Mount Horeb, there was a man by the name of Moses who in reverie was keeping the sheep of his father-in-law, Jethro. And as he sat there alone, suddenly he became aware of a phenomenon that was beyond his experience. He saw a bush that burned and was not consumed. And as he went to draw near, God spoke to him.

Let me read it for you; in the third chapter of the book of Exodus, there is this word: "God called unto him out of the midst of the bush, and said, Moses, Moses. . . . Draw not nigh hither: put off thy shoes from off thy feet, for the place whereon thou standest is holy ground. . . . I am the God of . . . Abraham, the God of Isaac, and the God of Jacob. And Moses hid his face . . . and Jehovah said, I have surely seen the affliction of my people . . . and have heard their cry by reason of their taskmasters; for I know their sorrows; and I am come down to deliver them." But all of this was addressed to the man Moses and the name was repeated: "Moses, Moses."

Or go with me much later to Shiloh and to the tabernacle of God, to the days when Eli was the high priest. Remember there was a little lad who didn't know the Lord, who had been left at Shiloh to tend the needs of Eli and to be instructed and trained by the high priest. His name was Samuel, and God spoke to Samuel; and Samuel didn't know who it was that spoke to him. You remember the story, how he went to Eli, thinking it was Eli who spoke to him. And Eli finally, after that Samuel had come to him three times, said to him, "It's the Lord, and this is the way you shall answer." You'll see it in chapter 3 of the book of 1 Samuel and verse 10. "And Jehovah came, and stood, and called as at other times, Samuel, Samuel. Then Samuel said, Speak; for thy servant heareth." It seems to be a custom of the Lord to repeat the name.

Sometimes He doesn't. I remember in the scene in the garden at the time of the resurrection, when Mary stood alone; and she went and looked into the tomb and saw two angels in white apparel, one at the head and one at the foot of the tomb; and the tomb was empty. And she turned around to leave the tomb, and she was aware that someone whom she thought was the gardener was standing there. And the angel said, "Why weepest thou?" And she gave the answer, thinking the Lord was the gardener; she said, "Where have you laid him?" Then the Lord said just one word: He said, "Mary." Oh, that I could have the intonation and the modulation of voice to express it the way He did. For immediately, she knew who it was. And immediately she said, "Rabboni," my Teacher, my Master.

You remember how that on the shores of the lake of Galilee the disciples had gathered, and the Lord was there; and the Lord invited them to come from their fishing, and He said, "Simon, son of John, lovest thou me?"

So He's coming someday. I believe He'll call us by name. "My love, my fair one." I remember a verse I was taught by my mother that even as a lad, brought great comfort to my heart, and through the years, again and again, God has used it to quiet my soul and to give rest to my spirit. Listen to it: "Fear not, I have redeemed thee, I have called thee by thy name, thou art mine." The Lord knows our names. We are of more value than many sparrows, and even the very hairs of our head are numbered. And so when He comes again, there's going to be the expression of an invitation: "Rise up, my love, my fair one, and come away."

There is a second thing here: the expression of the cessation of trial, beautifully expressed, "For, lo, the winter is past; The rain is over and gone; The flowers appear on the earth; The time of the singing of birds is come, And the voice of the turtle-dove is heard in our land." The winter is past; the rain is over and gone. Haven't you ever longed for the winter to be past? Haven't you ever, from the depths of your heart, cried out to God for the end of the rain? He's going to say, when He comes again, "The winter is past, the rain is over and gone."

Friends of mine are rather critical of David, when in the

fifty-fifth psalm, it is recorded that he said, "Oh that I had wings like a dove, Then would I fly away, and be at rest." Long since, I've given up any criticism of David for that. I've been there myself. Oh, that I had the wings of a dove! Bless your heart, someday He's coming, and the winter will be past; the rains will be over and gone. The winter with all its cold and blasted hopes, long nights, will be ended; and the rains of adversity, the storms of distress, the torrents of grief and of tears will be over and gone. When He comes again, "the winter is past," He'll say, "The rains are over and gone."

> The sands of time are sinking,
> The dawn of Heaven breaks;
> The summer morn I've sighed for,
> The fair sweet morn awakes.
> Dark, dark hath been the midnight,
> But dayspring is at hand,
> And glory, glory dwelleth
> In Immanuel's land.

I'm speaking to some of you, and you're passing through the valley, and you're tempted to be despondent. May I remind you, the Lord is coming; and when the Lord comes, the winter is past, and the rain is over and gone. And then we'll be able to say, in the lovely words of Samuel Rutherford.

> With mercy and with judgment
> My web of time He wove,
> And aye the dews of sorrow
> Were lustered by His love;
> I'll bless the hand that guided,
> I'll bless the heart that planned,
> When throned where glory dwelleth,
> In Immanuel's land.

Oh, there's so much I don't understand now. There's so much I can't explain. I found out early in my ministry that I had no answers for many of the trials and testings that came to my people except: God knows; God cares. And even if I can't prove it, it is so, that He makes all things work together for good. I remember the first time I turned to a dear soul deep in bereavement and said, "The verse says, 'we know,' not, 'we understand'; we know that all things work together." And we know it not because we can dissect it, not because we can analyze it, not because we have smooth answers for all the questions unbelievers ask; no, we know it because we know Him, that's why. And He cannot be false to any of His children. The winter is past, the rain is over and gone.

But, may I in faithfulness say to you that's not all that will be over and gone. Thank God, we're looking for heaven and the presence of the Lord, but we have some privileges now that are going to be over when He comes. May I remind you that you will not increase in faith after you've seen Him, because faith will give place to sight. You'll no longer be able to sing,

> 'Tis so sweet to trust in Jesus,
> Just to take Him at His word,
> Just to rest upon His promise,
> Just to know, "Thus saith the Lord."
> Jesus, Jesus, how I trust Him,
> How I've proved Him o'er and o'er!
> Jesus, Jesus precious Jesus,
> Oh, for grace to trust Him more!

But you see, you're going to be home; and all that you have in faith will come to pass. Oh, how God speaks to me about this. I have the privilege even in the dark hours of earth's experience to put my hand in the hand of my Father and say, "Even so, Father, for it seemeth right in thine eyes."

God wants, God longs to be trusted. He that cometh to God must believe, must believe that He is, and that He's a rewarder of them that diligently seek Him. But you'll not need to have faith, because it's all realized in the glory. That's the reason God speaks to my own heart again and again that when He allows trial to come and testing to come and William Culbertson begins to groan and grieve and complain, I hear my Father say, "Son, this is your opportunity of opportunities to walk with Me and to know My presence the way you'll never know it in any other experience." Increase of faith will be over.

Growth in grace will be over, because when we see Him we shall be like Him. But oh, the thrilling exhilaration of walking day by day with the Lord and finding that He's leading me on in the knowledge of Himself and in fellowship with Himself. Growth in grace ends in perfection, for then we shall know even as we are known.

Bless God, I have some privileges now, and even though my eyes are blinded with tears, and even though I have no explanation for what the Lord has allowed to come into my life in the way of suffering and trial, this I know: I can trust Him and He'll be pleased. It's easy to go along when things are well; but oh, when the dark clouds come, and when the night comes, just to walk with Him. I'd rather walk in the dark with God than walk alone in the light. I think you know what I'm talking about, those of you who know me. Increase in faith is over when He comes, because where you and I shall be by the grace of God, only saved people will be. The winter is past, the rain is over and gone. And all the heartaches and all the sorrow will be over.

One thing more. It is the expression of deepest love and holiest ardor. Think of Him, think of the Lord saying to you and to me: "my love, my fair one." Think of Him saying, "O my dove, that art in the clefts of the rock, In the covert of the steep place, Let me see thy countenance, Let me hear thy voice; For sweet is thy voice, and thy countenance is comely."

I was greatly blessed years ago in reading in *Daily Light* the selection for the day of April tenth. The family that brought together the texts for *Daily Light* brought together texts in contrast for that day. Listen to them; this is my confession: "Behold, I was shapen in iniquity, and in sin did my mother conceive me." But what does my lovely Lord say to me? That's my confession; that's true of William Culbertson naturally, but what does He say? This is what He says: "Thy renown went forth among the heathen for thy beauty, for it was perfect through my comeliness which I had put upon thee, saith the Lord God." My confession, His evaluation. Again, my confession: "I am a sinful man, O Lord." What does He see as He sees me? "Behold, thou art fair, my love; behold thou art fair." My confession: "I abhor myself, and repent in dust and ashes." But His word is: "Thou art all fair, my love, there is no spot in thee." Hallelujah! The blood of Jesus Christ, God's Son, keeps on cleansing us from all sin. So, thank God for this expression of deepest love. Listen, "Sweet is thy voice," He says; "comely is thy countenance." Oh, the wonder of it, the grace of it! Do you wonder why I love Him? I think I have a number of favorite hymns, but none is more meaningful to me than the worship and adoration expressed first of all by Bernard of Clairvaux in these words:

> Oh Jesus, King most wonderful,
> Thou Counsellor renowned,
> Thou sweetness most ineffable,
> From Whom all joys abound.

He's coming again, and He's going to say, "Sweet is thy voice, comely is thy countenance."

I trust that this isn't just theoretical with you. The blessed Lord is coming. And when He comes there'll be the expression of an invitation and the expression of the cessation of trial, and the expression of deepest love and holiest ardor. I must close with this word. I quote Samuel Rutherford again:

> The bride eyes not her garment,
> But her dear bridegroom's face;
> I will not gaze at glory,
> But on my King of grace;
> Not at the crown He giveth,
> But on His pierced hands;
> The Lamb is all the glory
> Of Immanuel's land.

Let us pray.

We love thee, Lord Jesus. Thou hast first loved us and given Thyself to us. How we long for the day when this same Jesus shall so come in like manner as the disciples saw Him go into heaven, when the Lord Himself shall descend from heaven with a shout. Make, we pray Thee, this doctrine blessed to us, meaningful to us. May we live in the light of it: our lovely Lord is coming again. We pray in the name of the Lord Jesus, Amen.